The
Journey
To
Me

Finding Freedom in the Inconvenient
Realities of Existence

Annette Birkmann

The
Journey
To
Me

Finding Freedom in the Inconvenient
Realities of Existence

Translated by James Bulman-May

Copyright © 2024 by Annette Birkmann

The Journey to Me
is translated from Danish from *Rejsen til mig*

Translation by James Bulman-May
First printing / edition 2024
Cover Design and Typesetting by Trisha Fuentes
Maps: Remote Grafik

ISBN: 978-87-995288-2-0

All rights reserved.

Copying from this book is permitted only in compliance with the rules of applicable copyright law.

OpenRoad Publishing

Begin to be aware of your present condition whatever that condition is. Stop being a dictator. Stop trying to push yourself somewhere. Then someday you will understand that simply by awareness you have already attained what you were pushing yourself toward.

ANTHONY DE MELLO

CONTENTS

Foreword 1
Introduction. 5

Chapter 1 The Leap 7
Have no Expectations

Chapter 2 Baggage 23
Let Go

Chapter 3 Planning A Route 51
Listen to Yourself

Chapter 4 Riding Techniques. 75
Engage Fully

Chapter 5 The Low Point. 111
Be Alone

Chapter 6 Protection 133
Be Disarming

Chapter 7 Problem-Solving. 151
Be Honest

Chapter 8 Accidents 171
Surrender

Chapter 9 The Finish Line 201
Share your Joy

Afterword
Acknowledgements
Help Shape The Journey

FOREWORD

On a crisp, late afternoon in spring, my dog and I had settled into a quiet camping spot along a small mountainside in rural Mississippi in the southeastern part of the United States, when with a quiet rush a motorcyclist pulled in nearby. The lone rider quickly unpacked gear and set up a small tent. Being a social Southerner, I decided to offer my new neighbor a cold beer from an ice box in the back of my truck, and share some firewood.

To my pleasant surprise, the grateful traveler turned out to be one of the most easy-going yet quietly intense women with whom I have crossed paths in my travels around the country and world. It was a synchronicity of fellow travelers sharing food, drink, and company while swapping amazing experiences from faraway lands beside a crackling open fire.

Yet her tale, only part of which is shared in this journal, gave me pause. I know that in between the insights and openness, which don't always come easily, were untold thoughts which she pondered, and feelings that were kept close to her amazed heart.

I wasn't surprised at any of this, not even her passion for her often-uncomfortable mode of travel, at least not at first. But it was obviously both challenging and exhilarating, this self-induced exile from her Other World. It was so much more than a mere adventure.

Within thirty-six hours, after much laughter and having delved quickly and deeply into local 'soul' food, a bouncing pick-up truck drive along the shores of the mighty Mississippi River, and late-night sharing of the haunting Blues music of the Mississippi Delta, Annette would be off again, continuing her solo journey of proving herself to herself.

This book is a sometimes-shy, often-defiant celebration of a lone human throwing physical comfort to the wind and taking to the Road, across many cultures in search of something elusive, and in the process becoming part of the road itself. Every unique individual Annette met, every simple meal she shared, every difficulty and every surprising discovery that came her way, has been a tipping point of sorts.

What little bits Annette is sharing in this journal have been cobbled into an age-old tale of a big heart and inquiring mind in search of... well, read on and ponder for yourself.

Felder Rushing
Author of Slow Gardening

Mexico City
MEXICO
GUATEMALA
HONDURAS
San José
COSTA RICA
Panama City
PANAMA
Bogotá
COLOMBIA
Quito
ECUADOR
PERU
Lima
BRAZIL
BOLIVIA
La Paz
PARAGUAY
Asunción
CHILE
URUGUAY
Santiago
Montevideo
Buenos Aires
ARGENTINA
1000 km

INTRODUCTION

Most of us have probably experienced the feeling of reaching a point in our lives when we pause to think: 'Was that it?'

Every time I have reached a goal in my life, it's been with the expectation that once this goal is achieved, everything would from then on be fine – I'll be free, I'll be happy. But things seldom worked out that way. I've never felt completely free or satisfied, or certainly not for any substantial length of time. Sooner or later my problems would catch up with me, zoning in like some over-zealous GPS.

When I got divorced at the age of thirty, I knew I needed a change of direction. I just had no idea where or how to begin.

Without a conscious motive or any expectation of future salvation, I decided to realise my childhood dream of riding a motorcycle. Eight months after getting my licence, I quit my job at a law office in Copenhagen, moved to Buenos Aires in Argentina, and took unpaid work at a motorcycle workshop to learn the art of motorcycle maintenance. When I arrived, I could neither speak Spanish nor did I know anything about the mechanics of bikes. I'd never even owned one.

In Buenos Aires, I bought my first model, a six-year-old black-and-white BMW F 650 GS Dakar, and after eight months at the workshop I set off by myself on a year-long road trip through Latin America.

A dream that exceeded my wildest imaginings had become a reality. There was no need to worry about money or obligations. Before departing,

I had sold most of my possessions. The house went during the divorce, and subsequently I sold my car and disposed of half my belongings. I had set myself free. For the first time in my life, I'd let myself do what felt right for me. So what could possibly go wrong now?

Well, quite a lot, as it turned out. Hence the book. As the workshop owner remarked the day before I left on my trip, 'Remember, if nothing goes wrong, you'll have nothing to narrate when you return.' In the end, having nothing to narrate wasn't something I had to worry about – it was actually one of the few things I didn't have to worry about during my year on South American roads.

I certainly don't regret undertaking a journey fraught with challenges. In fact, I'm grateful for every single obstacle that kept me on my toes. With challenges on all fronts, being kept under near-constant pressure, and, most importantly, having no one else to lean on, I was forced to learn new ways of dealing with the inconvenient realities of existence on the fly. It made me ask myself whether it's possible to find joy and freedom by realizing the goals and dreams we all set ourselves – and if not, then where indeed do they truly lie?

On the surface, it looked as though my decision to go to South America had changed my life. What's clear to me now, however, is that I'd simply restaged the drama of my life from Copenhagen to South America. I still thought and acted the same way as before, resulting in the same consequences.

What this book is about, then, is not simply a motorcycle trip through the Americas, but rather the inner journey I made at the same time. It taught me that the root cause of the external turmoil in my life thus far was primarily my inability to be consciously aware of my thoughts and feelings – without trying to soothe or control them. This awareness was the gist of the freedom and joy I'd been seeking, hitherto to no avail, in the world around me. This was the real takeaway from my many hours, days, weeks, and months on the bike.

CHAPTER 1

THE LEAP
Have no Expectations

> People look to time in expectation that it will eventually make them happy, but you cannot find true happiness by looking toward the future.
>
> ECKHART TOLLE

I was at a loss, not knowing what to do, feeling vexed and powerless. I felt as though my life had just spun out of control.

It happened on the morning of my thirtieth birthday. The marital spat that triggered an avalanche lasted only ten minutes, but it was ten days before he spoke to me again. When he did open his mouth, it was to say he'd quit his job. One year earlier, we'd bought a house north of Copenhagen, which we couldn't keep on a single income.

It was only after the argument that I realised how unhappy the man I lived with had become. He'd voiced his complaints and despite many of them being legitimate, I didn't listen. For several months, he'd been trying to tell me he wasn't happy in our marriage, but I didn't want to hear it. If I had started listening to him, I'd have been forced to listen to myself, which was even more terrifying than listening to him. I was simply afraid of discovering that I wasn't leading the life I wanted to live.

We tried to fix the damage through consultation with a couple's therapist. During the sessions, we were sitting three feet from each other in a basement room in a villa north of Copenhagen, albeit with the feeling of a vast gulf separating us. Opposite sat a man who asked us to commit to words our latent feelings. I don't exactly remember what was said, but I do faintly recall a palpable feeling of anger, resignation, and grief. After three visits to the therapist, we left with only the vague sensation of having been heard by each other.

Until that point, I hadn't considered divorce as an option. I couldn't imagine anything scarier than getting divorced – I doubted I had the strength to go through the changes it would bring. If it were up to me, I'd do anything to avoid finding out what was hiding behind the facade of that villa.

However, the evening after our last visit to the therapist, as I examined myself in the bathroom mirror, I suddenly thought, 'Oh shit. What if we succeed in saving our marriage?'

The quarrel and its aftermath had set something in motion that was beyond my power to control. I caught a hint of it when I was busy tidying up some boxes of old letters and found in it a scrap of paper from a woman I'd worked with in England after high school. It was a quotation in Italian – *Nel mezzo del cammin di nostra vita mi ritrovai per una selva oscura ché la diritta via era smarrita* – with an additional line in English: 'Maybe for now, but nothing lasts forever.'

I'd had that note for twelve years, and it had never occurred to me to find out its meaning. I turned to a former student friend, half-Danish and half-Italian, and sought for a translation. It turned out to be the opening lines of Dante's *Divine Comedy*. It said: 'Midway upon the journey of our life / I found myself within a forest dark, / For the straight-forward pathway had been lost.'

A month and a half later, while my husband was abroad for a week, I printed out the divorce papers from the local authority website and signed them. When he got back, I took them out and asked him to sign them. He did so without objection.

I'd reached a point where I'd rather lose everything than remain in our marriage. Even though I didn't trust myself to navigate life, often ignoring my inner alarm bells because of it, I needed to go on alone.

I'd been living in accordance with (the unconscious) belief that it was more important to fit in than to be true to myself. I'd accomplished the goals I'd set myself without considering whether they were the right ones for me, desperate to avoid ownership of my thoughts and feelings at any cost. Not knowing how to express my thoughts and feelings persuasively and be heard, it was easier to keep them to myself and adapt to my surroundings. I adapted myself in a way that superficially looked like I'd gained the acceptance of my surroundings, hoping it could replace the fact that I didn't acknowledge my own thoughts and feelings.

Being steered by external circumstances, I hadn't developed the ability to listen to myself and move towards making healthy choices. That had negative consequences not just for myself but also for those around me, and my marriage was no exception. I often said yes when I meant no, and vice versa. I was afraid of being rejected if I faced up to myself. It was safer to hide my vulnerability and the emotional tumult within, which stretched from mild restlessness and unease to a sense of teetering on the edge of an abyss.

For many years I'd tried to deaden this inner sense of unease by overeating, smoking, partaking of alcohol, watching TV, surfing on the internet, shopping – you name it. The specific activity didn't really matter, so long as it distracted my attention from the black hole within me. But the emotional turmoil continued to grow, and the tactics to tame it grew less and less effective.

Six weeks after signing the divorce papers, I met a man whom I believed could fill the dark void. Although it didn't work out, the encounter did set me on a new course in my life.

I was in Berlin for a conference, and upon entering the conference hall, I caught sight of a man in the back row. I saw him from the side and fell in love with him in a heartbeat. I found a place further forward, where I sat struggling with the temptation to turn around and stare until an image formed in my mind of a house for sale, a soon-to-be ex-husband, and a stack of unsolved problems. It did put a damper on my urge to gawk, and I finally decided to avoid all contact with the man.

During the break, I went out into the lobby and poured myself a cup of coffee. I wasn't interested in mingling, and yet I felt awkward as I stood there staring vacantly into space. It seemed as though my life were in ruins. For the time being I had no notion of who I was. For sure, I could reel off the obvious – name, gender, occupation – but apart from that, I was drawing a blank.

It wasn't long, however, before the man from the hall came up to me and initiated a conversation. I understood he was half South American and half European, plus a few details about his job – that was all. The attraction was too strong for me to listen minutely to what he was saying. The fascination didn't merely weaken my hearing. In fact, it shut down whatever minimal cerebral activity might have been involved. The noises that came out of my mouth probably didn't make me sound too bright.

We ended up spending the weekend together in Berlin, and at no point during that period did my feet touch the ground. My hearing never got over that first blow and I still don't remember what we talked about. The only thing that stuck was a remark about how he was going back to South America the following year.

I returned to Copenhagen transformed into a different person. Our encounter had struck a chord in me that had been dead since my marriage – I felt desire, and I felt free. For the first time in a long while I felt alive. Stark-raving-madly alive. I couldn't keep calm and had only one immediate goal in head: namely, to see him again.

My desire, however, was not requited. Outwardly, I respected that, but inside I was convinced we'd get together eventually – sooner or later. Preferably sooner if I had anything to do with it. So, two and a half months after our meeting in Berlin, I booked a plane ticket to South America in the irrational hope of bumping into him by chance. I couldn't bring myself to contact him to find out whether – and, if so, where, and when – he might be there.

Our meeting had put me back in touch with myself, and I discovered that primarily what I needed was to get away from home to put my life in perspective. At the same time, I urgently wanted to go somewhere I hadn't been before, and where I didn't know anybody.

I hadn't previously considered South America. It had never interested me, and it certainly wasn't a place I wanted to explore alone. Yet, on New Year's Eve, I found myself on a plane, heading into unknown territory, without a companion or an itinerary.

Without expectation

A decision to do something without being motivated by the hope that it will bring future happiness opens new possibilities.

On my way to South America with my rucksack upon my back, I'd blocked two months out of the calendar as part of a change of employment.

Salar de Uyuni, Bolivia.

My trip started in Rio de Janeiro in Brazil and continued to Buenos Aires in Argentina – a city with which I fell head-over-heels in love. Its melancholic, yet dramatic atmosphere was congenial to my troubled emotional state, and I had a sense of freedom there.

From Buenos Aires I went to Salta in northern Argentina, incidentally ending up on a bus to San Pedro de Atacama in Chile, where I struck up a pleasant conversation with two fellow travelers. Together, we took a three-day jeep trip through the salt flats of Salar de Uyuni in Bolivia.

I'd never imagined such enchanting landscapes existed on earth. It offered an unmistakable feeling of landing on another planet, at once surrounded by red and turquoise lakes, hot springs, and rock formations that looked like Dali sculptures, with the Andes' golden peaks and the deep-blue sky as a backcloth. A two-day journey through this alien landscape brought us to a small island, Isla Incahuasi, in the middle of the salt flats, at an elevation of 12,000 feet. Here I found a quiet and tranquil corner away from other travellers.

I let the silence and the plateau's wild beauty envelop me, as I gazed across the salt plain covering an area of one quarter of Denmark. My mind was still and my body – my hands, especially – hummed with life as though I'd fallen deeply in love. Suddenly, out of the blue, I recalled my childhood dream of riding a motorcycle. Every spring and every autumn, when the Bakken Amusement Park north of Copenhagen opened and closed, I would stand on Strandvejen, the beach road north of Copenhagen, and watch the motorcycles. Until I turned eighteen and left home, almost every year I would watch them ride past, wistfully imagining that one day I'd be one among them.

Riding a motorcycle is the earliest childhood dream I can recall and the only one that has lingered in my mind. As a teenager, I dreamt of flying fighter jets after watching the film Top Gun. That, however, didn't last. The motorcycles were different though. When I turned fifteen, I got a moped licence, but that was as far as I went. While studying law, I went on an exchange trip to Berlin, where a few of my German friends rode motorcycles. They let me try, and from the very first moment, I was crazy about it.

On the Bolivian salt flats, I realised I'd never get that licence, if I didn't do it now, and I promised myself I'd take the first steps when I got back from South America. The intent was not to change something in my life, or to embellish my CV, but rather that I wished to do it simply because it felt right for me.

A month later, I was back in Copenhagen and had started on a new job at a solicitor's office in Bredgade, a central address in the old part of Copenhagen. On my new route to and from work, I biked past a motorcycle riding school.

Salar de Uyuni, Bolivia.

Each day I passed the school without stopping to sign up or taking time to compare the fees at other schools. After a week I'd got no further. On the following day, as I cycled past the school, I recalled the promise I'd made myself in Bolivia, and at that very moment of desperation or perhaps clarity, I said to myself: 'Hell no – I'm doing it now! Even if it be the worst and most expensive school in Copenhagen. I'm going inside and putting my name down.'

Three months later, I had in my possession my motorcycle licence. When I took the practical test, it felt as though I was flying. Now all I needed were two wheels and a motor.

Shortly afterward, I had dinner with a good friend and former colleague. One of our favorite topics of conversation back then was what we would do if we weren't working in law. I told him about my yearning to travel to South America, ride a motorcycle and learn Spanish, but I couldn't figure out how to make it happen. 'Why don't you do all three things at the same time?' my friend suggested.

For the first time in my life, I knew without a shred of doubt what I should do, even though it made barely any sense. Giving up my well-paying job, scuppering my legal career, and selling off most of my possessions seemed a crazy idea that felt right. Yet strangely, there was no sense of fear at the prospect of taking the necessary steps. A brief encounter with a handsome South American man and a conversation with a good friend had set in motion something bigger than me.

The following week I asked for two weeks' holiday in late summer and bought a plane ticket to Buenos Aires. My plan was to hire a motorcycle and discover if I liked (and could handle) riding alone around South America.

I boarded the plane with my new motorcycle licence, a borrowed motorcycle jacket, and the address of a motorcycle rental company.

The day after I arrived, I went down to the rental company. I'd be lying if I said I wasn't nervous as I sat in the taxi – I knew nothing about the place or the people who ran it. In Denmark, certain motorcyclists have a dodgy reputation, and this was Buenos Aires. I could scarcely imagine what kind of bikers they had here.

'Motocare' was written in big yellow letters on an orange background. A row of motorcycles was parked out front. I paid the taxi driver, got out and eyed the business from a safe distance. No danger in sight – a good start. I crossed the road and went inside. The place was over-filled with motorcycles of all descriptions. A bald man, who looked more like a gangster, was sitting behind a messy desk, talking to a customer. The moment they saw me, they abruptly stopped, and an awkward silence ensued. Evidently, they didn't get many female customers from Scandinavia.

The bald man greeted me in Spanish. Mustering my courage, I stammered out my few well-rehearsed Spanish words: *Quisiera alquilar una moto.* I'd like to rent a motorcycle. The bald man gave a lengthy answer in Spanish. When the stream of language came to a halt, I explained in English that I didn't understand Spanish. Our conversation continued in the same vein until he picked up the telephone, dialed a number and handed me the receiver. I stared at the cordless phone like I'd never seen one before. Only when the man said 'speak' did I put it to my ear and say a cautious 'hello.'

To my relief, I heard a voice speaking fluent English. It turned out to be the owner of Motocare, Mariano. He asked if I could wait ten minutes, and he'd come down to the office. Given that it had taken me twenty hours to get to Buenos Aires, I could see no grounds for objection.

Rented Honda, Buenos Aires.

North of Mendoza, Argentina.

From the first time I saw Mariano, I was in no doubt that I could rely upon him entirely. His gaze was steady and his smile disarming and obliging, and I instinctively sensed he would do all he could to make my motorcycle trip in Argentina a good experience. Half an hour later I'd rented a Honda Transalp 600 for ten days and supplemented the equipment I'd brought with a loaned helmet, motorcycling trousers and a pair of gloves. Two days later I picked up the bike and, scared out of my wits, put it into gear and headed west out of the city.

The motorcycle trip across Argentina had a buoyant effect on me, making me feel free, vibrant, and happy beyond words. It was only later that it struck me that this was so. It was as if I'd been uprooted and bunged into a road movie, in which every swerve worked on my self-image. I spent all ten days alone with my bike and Robert Pirsig's *Zen and the Art of Motorcycle Maintenance.*

Though the trip was a success, when I got home, I realised it had sapped away my energies. I'd challenged myself fundamentally and a bit beyond my capacity, so much so that my body reacted with physical symptoms. I spent two weeks in bed with a high fever, sleeping most of the time, while I tried to digest my Argentinian motorcycling adventure.

As the fever raged, I got so worried I called a psychologist I'd spoken to during the divorce. I explained my situation and plans to quit my job, asking if she thought I was going crazy. At the other end of the line, I heard a dry but heartening laugh. She told me the fear I was experiencing was normal and to be expected in a situation like mine, where I was busily pulling the rug out from beneath my own feet.

The reassurance that I wasn't going crazy after all improved my mood. A few weeks after the fever had subsided, I told my employer I'd be leaving, once I'd taken the bar exam.

On my journey across Argentina, I'd caught a glimpse of how my life could be if I dared be true to myself and fling myself into the things I yearned to do – even though they might go wrong. It occurred to me that I'd built my sense of safety on things outside myself – my titles, achievements, possessions and, not least, my marriage. In doing so, I'd deadlocked myself, but when my marriage floundered, my vulnerability was exposed. Here my CV was no help, and that realization made it possible for me to wrench myself free of the goals I'd set for myself to prove my worth.

All my life I'd tried to fight the feeling of vulnerability, but regardless of what I did, nothing worked as was clearly demonstrated through my divorce. Back then I was under the misconception that this vulnerability concealed a defect within me, perhaps a weak core or a black hole that could destroy me.

I didn't realize that the feeling of vulnerability was simply part and parcel of being human, regardless of what you do or where you are – that it was something I had to figure out how to live with. All I knew was that my attempts to feel safe by fitting in hadn't worked. I was still stuck feeling vulnerable, so I might as well take a plunge into doing the things I longed to do.

A few days after quitting my job, I sat in my office looking at the case files on my desk. Instead of picking up a file, I thought of the leap I'd just begun to make. To be capable of travelling alone through South America on a motorcycle, I had to learn something about the mechanics of bikes. I also needed – and wanted – to learn Spanish. Without thinking twice, I wrote an email to Mariano at the motorcycle shop in Buenos Aires, asking if he knew of a place down there, where I could learn to fix bikes. The very next day, I received his response:

'Your question is easy to answer. You can learn the most common aspects of motorcycle maintenance in our shop if you're interested – and if you think you can handle it.' 'If you think you can handle it?' What in the world did he mean by that? Of course, I can handle it, I thought.

Four months later I'd deposited my newly acquired certification as a solicitor with the Ministry of Justice, subleased my apartment, and was standing outside my new workplace, a motorcycle garage in Buenos Aires. If anybody had told me one year earlier that I'd be standing there, I'd have sworn they were crazy. However, as I looked at the facade and all the bikes displayed in the window, it felt as if it had always been part of the plan.

It would be more than twenty-five years before I fulfilled my childhood dream of being one of the motorcyclists on the road to Bakken. But before that dream came true, I rode 33,000 miles all by myself through the vast continents of South and North America on a motorcycle. People have often asked me how it started, and my response is simply that I listened to my heart and took the first step with no expectation that it would change my life.

Riding a motorcycle wasn't a means for me to reach an end. It was the activity itself – riding the bike – that was the goal, no matter where it took me. Precisely because my decision to get a licence wasn't connected to any expectation that it would bring me future happiness (it made me happy already), I was open to the possibilities that arose and capable of acting on the ones that felt right for me.

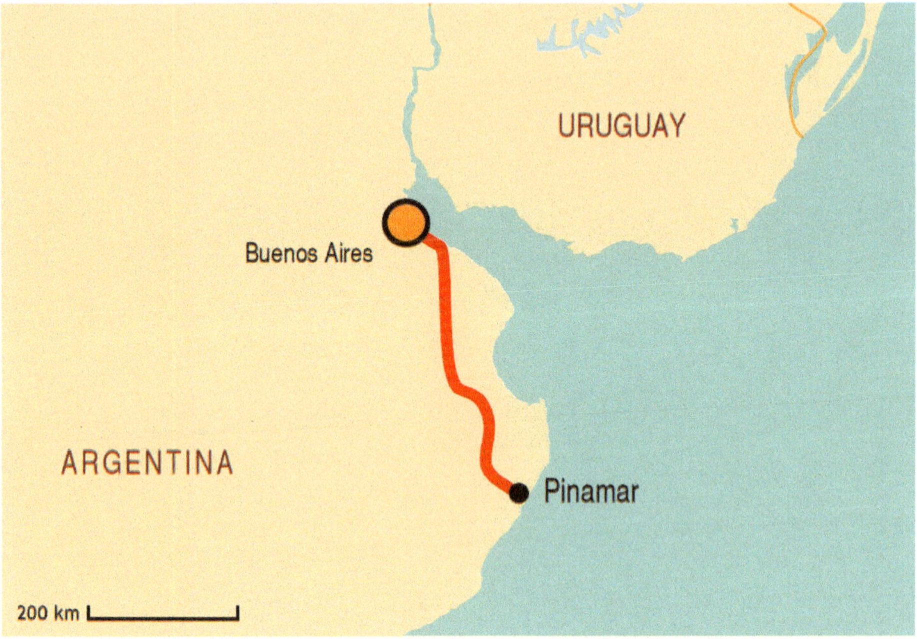
URUGUAY
Buenos Aires
ARGENTINA
Pinamar
200 km

CHAPTER 2

BAGGAGE
Let Go

> The real voyage of discovery consists, not in seeking new landscapes, but in having new eyes.
>
> MARCEL PROUST

On a longer motorcycle trip, one should carry as little luggage as possible. The less weight you have on the motorcycle, the easier it is to handle, and the lower the risk of accidents.

If it dawns on me along the way that I am missing something, whatever it may be, I will be able to find something that can meet my needs. It could well be that I may have to take a detour, or perhaps that what I find isn't exactly what I had in mind. However, if I really need it, I will be able to get that too. If I can't find what I am looking for, then probably I don't need it.

That may necessitate a change of plans. If I am not willing to do that, I will be stuck. It's just important to understand that the reason I'm stuck isn't that I didn't find what I needed. I'm stuck because I'm unwilling to change my plans. This applies not only to a motorcycle trip but also to life in general.

It's important to be aware that there are two types of luggage: physical luggage and mental and emotional luggage. Excessive physical luggage is undoubtedly a nuisance, but what usually overturns the load is the mental and emotional baggage, so let me start here.

The inner baggage

I arrived in Buenos Aires on a Sunday morning in the month of April and took a taxi from the airport to the motorcycle shop where Mariano was waiting. He had arranged for me to stay with Diego – also called Pelado (the bald man) – who was the gangster-looking man I had met the first time I set foot in the store. Diego lived opposite Motocare and here I could stay until I found my own apartment. A Finnish acquaintance who lived in Buenos Aires put me in touch with someone who arranged rentals, and after two weeks, I had rented an apartment in the affluent Recoleta neighborhood, close to the famous cemetery where Eva Peron is buried.

Although the selection of apartments in Buenos Aires was large, it was not difficult to choose. I needed an apartment with a parking space for my future motorcycle, and there weren't too many of them. When I was shown a furnished apartment with a parking space in the basement, a swimming pool on the shared roof terrace, and for a rent that equaled the price of a dormitory room in Denmark, I immediately jumped at the chance.

The first few weeks in my new city I spent trying to fully grasp that I had taken the leap away from the law firm in Denmark and apparently had landed on my feet in a motorcycle shop on the South American continent. It was like exiting a familiar world and entering a very different, unfamiliar, one. Not only did the physical workplaces differ from each other, my colleagues and customers seemed to hail from different planets.

Diego, Mariano and Sergio in the workshop (the other Diego (Pelado) is not in the photo), Buenos Aires.

I had four colleagues in the motorcycle shop: the owner, Mariano, who spoke fluent English, and three younger Argentine men who spoke only Spanish. When I showed up on the first day, it dawned on me that I was not the only one who had been looking forward to my arrival – I could barely recognize the shop. The desk was cleared, the workshop was clean, and each wrench hung in its place. Mariano had even asked the mechanic, Sergio, to mix cement and patch a hole in the back-room floor.

After the introduction to my new colleagues, I was left in the back room with Sergio, who put a cup of mate in my hand – a very bitter herbal tea that is popular in Argentina. Sergio then set about repairing a rather large mechanical construction, while explaining in Spanish what he was doing.

Half an hour later, Mariano came by and stopped Sergio's attempt to explain to me how a carburettor works. He instead suggested that Sergio show me how to take a wheel off a motorcycle. Using the tried and tested "monkey see, monkey do" technique, I soon fell into the rhythm of the motorcycle workshop, far away from anything similar I had done before.

I enjoyed being away from the routine of deskwork and staring at a computer screen. It was fun to help Sergio in the workshop and learn about various motorcycle parts and tools. For the first few weeks, I didn't understand much of what he said. We communicated using my pocket dictionary. When the limit of the use of the word 'sorry' was reached, I had two strategies: Either I pretended I had understood what was said (adding appropriate sounds to support this), and when this didn't work, I bluntly admitted my ignorance. This always elicited a smile from Sergio, who handled it accommodatingly with *no pasa nada* or *no importa* – it doesn't matter or it's not important.

Spanish was the first Romance language I learned, and it was pretty far removed from the languages I had learned in school. I had a hard time grasping that it was necessary with to verbs for 'to be' and a specific verb for every possible movement. Why not say 'going up' and 'going down' instead of *subir* and *bajar*? In the morning, I went to a language school to learn the many verbs and conjugations, and in the afternoon, I learned in the workshop the words that weren't part of the curriculum at school. By this, I mean not only words for motorcycle parts but also Spanish-Argentine slang of the rude kind. My vocabulary in this area flourished to such an extent that even my language teachers were impressed.

Not only was I challenged by the language and my new job, where I had no prerequisites or experience, and living in a big city in an unfamiliar part of the world. For the first few weeks, it was shocking to be confronted with the extreme poverty that exists in the city. On the streets and especially in the

In the workshop with Sergio, Buenos Aires.

subway, I saw people, often disabled, or deformed, who begged or peddlers who sold pens, plastic gadgets, and paper napkins.

In the evening, the poor from the many *villas miserias*, as the slums in Argentina are called, came to the city to collect waste such as glass and cardboard for recycling. Once a week, my neighbors and I put our trash in front of the building, and late at night the poor people came with large pushcarts to sort and pick up the rubbish on the pavement. Then they went back to the outlying areas in an old train reserved for the recycling hunters, where they sold the waste for recycling.

Not only was this sight of poverty foreign to me, but the Argentine culture was also far removed from the Danish. The significant class differences divided the city into an A- and a B-team who don't mix – as a European, I was ascribed to the A-team.

Moreover, there were social conventions, which were unfamiliar to me. I cannot exactly put my finger on what gave me the feeling of speaking past the Argentines. Part of the confusion was of course due to the language, while on the other hand I was overwhelmed by new impressions that I had to navigate.

Just a walk in the supermarket could take an hour – not only because I had a hard time finding the items I was looking for, but also because of the slow process at the till. The clerk had to put all banknotes under ultraviolet light or up against the ceiling light to determine their authenticity, and then there was almost always a lack of change. Lack of change was a widespread phenomenon in the supermarkets in Buenos Aires. I have spent a total of many hours in queues when a clerk shouted: *cambio* (change).

Nevertheless, there was also a naivety and ignorance about the cultural codes, especially regarding male and female roles, which made me often wonder about people's reactions. It seemed like games between the sexes, which I wasn't used to from Denmark and therefore didn't understand. It had surprised me, for example, that the boys at Motocare had also been looking forward to my arrival. I had not given it a thought as the excitement about my new adventure failed to accommodate any other reactions until I faced them.

I felt and even looked different from the people around me. As a tall, fair-haired woman, I stood out no matter where I was in the city. When I bought myself a motorcycle, my appearance became no less striking. For example, one evening when I was leaving an Italian restaurant, five waiters came to the window to look at me while I was getting on my motorcycle. It got my pulse racing because I was afraid of dropping the bike and living up to the prejudices about women and vehicles that were much more prevalent in Argentina than in Denmark.

Traffic in Buenos Aires.

It was not easy to find Argentine friends. I had one though, who was Pelado's girlfriend, Yanina, who had immediately welcomed me. I had fun with the boys at Motocare, but we didn't meet up outside of work. My Finnish acquaintance was kind enough to invite me to dinners and city trips with his Finnish friends, but while I enjoyed their company, I never felt part of the group.

A few months after my arrival, I therefore joined Club Europeo. Here I would have a sanctuary being part of a mixed group of foreigners from Europe – or so I thought. For it turned out that most of the club members were Argentines with European grandparents. Some of them had never even set foot in Europe.

The club had several activities. There was the classic 'Drinks & Mingling,' which for the most part was a dating scene for Argentine, well-groomed women seeking a European man, and Argentine men looking for well-groomed women regardless of nationality. In addition, there were tango lessons. I signed up for them, but it was no success.

First, it was difficult – really difficult. Second, I wasn't particularly crazy about tango music; I liked the modern, electronic tango music that *Gotan Project* and *Bajofondo* played, but we didn't dance to it. And third, there was my dance partner.

In the first lesson, we stood in two long rows, ladies, and gentlemen separately. Our tango teacher then put us together in pairs. I was one of the last to be assigned a partner, and when the teacher introduced us, he looked at me with wide eyes and let his gaze run from the tips of my shoes to the top of my head, which was 15 inches taller than him. "You want me to dance with her?" he exclaimed in horror. Yes, but not for long. I felt like an elephant next to him.

The biggest challenge in Buenos Aires, though, was dealing with the mental baggage I had dragged with me from home. Shortly after I arrived, I was controlled by the same thought and action patterns that I had hoped to leave behind at home.

Before I left, I was convinced that my dissatisfaction and inner turmoil had arisen because I had ended up on the wrong shelf. The one with the weekly publications of rulings and articles, trinkets from fancy design shops and a framed picture from the big wedding party. By placing myself on another shelf – or perhaps in my case by jumping completely out of the bookshelf – I thought that I could free myself from the shackles of this inner turmoil and dissatisfaction.

I wanted to get away from the pursuit of status and material goods that characterized my life in Denmark. I no longer wanted to dress nicely to go to work, hide under expensive brands or spend time shopping to build a self-image that really had nothing to do with me.

My steadfastness lasted two weeks, after which I ventured out shopping for the first time. I bought a skirt, a blouse, a handbag, and a pair of long boots with a heel. A few weeks later, I started applying mascara and lip gloss before going to work in the workshop.

At home in Denmark, I was close to being 'index 100'. In Denmark and the rest of Scandinavia, there are thousands of tall, fair-haired women, but in Buenos Aires I was unique and distinguished. Each time I received a compliment, it nurtured the desire for more.

Contrary to my intention, I had unwittingly started to replace the old layers with new ones. Now I was the tall, fair-haired lawyer from Denmark who rode a big motorcycle. Wasn't that cool? Pretty cool, I thought at the time, but it was just a new, empty shell.

Seeking attention from my surroundings was a placebo, an attempt at a quick fix or perhaps an escape from myself and the black hole within that made me more dissatisfied than before. And again, I began to ignore my own needs. Instead of planning my dream motorcycle journey, I was more concerned with pleasing others by trying to live up to what I thought was their idea of how I should be. The more attention I got, the more I believed I had managed to fit in.

I quickly lost interest in learning to repair motorcycles soon after the initial euphoria abated of being far away from the law. The excitement value of dirt under the fingernails has a limited lifespan – even in Buenos Aires.

After a month in the motorcycle shop, I started spending less time in the workshop and more time in front of the computer, surfing the web and writing emails to my family and friends. I also helped Mariano with translations and other paperwork. This way, my time in the workshop with Sergio was further reduced. The real purpose of working in the motorcycle shop – learning to repair motorcycles – receded into the background.

Purchasing the motorcycle

Only one thing managed to hold my attention and that was finding my first motorcycle. Even before I left Denmark, I knew the one I wanted: a BMW F 650 GS Dakar. I thought it was simply beautiful.

Arriving in Buenos Aires, I investigated the matter further. Upon consulting my new colleagues, my first instinct proved to be true. The BMW I had fallen in love with was ideal for the South American landscape. The only downside was the height of the seat, which for an inexperienced rider could be a challenge. The higher the seat, the higher the balance point, and consequently the harder it gets to handle the machine. It would make more sense to buy the standard version of this model, a BMW F 650 GS. It was identical to the Dakar model except for a lower seat height and a smaller front wheel.

It was not easy to find a used BMW F 650 GS for sale in Buenos Aires, even though I had my connections in order. After a month I had become impatient – I wanted to ride, so I signed up for a one-day motorcycle course at BMW to at least try my future motorcycle.

For the course, I could choose between the two models, but even though I was only interested in riding the Dakar model, I still asked the instructor for the standard version, expecting a note of dissuasion on grounds that I wouldn't be able to handle the Dakar model or that I would get hurt.

I got on the motorcycle, but was terribly disappointed, as it felt wrong. I could hardly have anticipated the shortcomings: the sitting position was uncomfortable, the engine was dull, and in the turns, it behaved like a bathtub on wheels. The motorcycle I initially thought would be the right one for me,

I did not like. My idea of the perfect motorcycle had thus been punctured, leaving me wondering whether I could trust my own reasoning.

The sharp contrast between my outer and inner reality meant that I fell into an old pattern: to rationalize and adapt my own experience to the idea in my head:

- My lack of experience as a rider is the reason for my disappointment.
- I had too high expectations.
- Other motorcycles are probably worse.
- I'm not paying attention.
- More experienced riders have told me that this is the right motorcycle for me. They obviously know better than I do.
- I shouldn't be so demanding.
- There's something wrong with me. Forget it and move on.

As the day progressed, these thoughts had convinced me that my own experience was wrong. A BMW F 650 GS was – whether I wanted it or not – the right motorcycle for me.

However, when we had ten minutes left of the course, I gave in to the urge to try the Dakar model. I had to know how it felt, if nothing else, to remove any doubt as to whether it could be the right motorcycle for me.

I sat up on the Dakar, kicked the side stand up, turned on the engine, and put it in gear. When I let go of the clutch and turned the throttle, I knew that instant I had found my motorcycle. The two models are almost identical, but for me, there was a world of difference. The Dakar was fun to ride, I enjoyed it, and I felt comfortable and safe. The instructor was in no doubt either – he could see that I had found my motorcycle, he said.

A few weeks later, Mariano found a six-year-old BMW F 650 GS Dakar for me. A lawyer who, in its first couple of years had logged 7,500 miles, had put it up for sale. Then he had had children, and since then it had been in the garage.

The cash payment was made in dollars, a thick wad of 100-dollar bills handed over in person to the seller at the public motor office, where the re-registration took place. There was no problem in this, as it were; the problem was to procure the thick wad of $100 bills in a volatile Argentine economy. I could not transfer the money to an Argentine bank if I wanted to be sure I could withdraw it again.

Here Mariano came to my aid again. The money was transferred via a bank in New York and to a company in Uruguay. I don't remember its name, but it was something like 'Company Inc.' – a company name that wouldn't have been approved by the Danish Business Authority. Then Mariano could go to an office in Buenos Aires (whose location is still unknown to me) and get the dollar bundle handed out – of course without showing an ID. We met with the lawyer at the public motor office, and half an hour later, the motorcycle was officially mine.

The next challenge was to ride my motorcycle in the asphalt jungle of Buenos Aires. I had noticed the heavy traffic, but it wasn't until I was in the middle of it all that it dawned upon me how crazy people were driving. For the first three weeks as a motorcycle rider in Buenos Aires, I woke up every morning asking myself: Is this the day I will die? I didn't experience much pleasure in riding in the beginning.

In fact, I didn't feel much joy at all in Buenos Aires. I was living my wildest dream and had just bought my dream motorcycle. During the first few months, admittedly, there were many moments filled with euphoria and a sense of freedom. However, those glimpses faded just about as quickly as they had formed. The black hole inside hadn't vanished, nor had it diminished.

First day as a motorcycle owner, at Motocare, Buenos Aires.

After three months in Buenos Aires, I sporadically began writing a diary, which I kept updating during my travels. During the year that I spent on my motorcycle journey through Latin America, it turned into a 500-page password-protected Word document. The password was to make sure no one could read a word I had written. The diary was my way of ridding myself of my innermost thoughts and feelings that I could share with no one else. For example – after five months in Buenos Aires – I concluded the day's report as follows:

> "Good night and sleep well!
> Ksfdhkjhskjhsgkjhskdjg = rage
> P.S.: I'm also dead tired of always being Miss Fucking Positive – because sometimes I'm just not fucking-oki-dokey fucking okay and positive – OKAY!?!?!?!"

I felt trapped by my usual dramas, and I had no idea how to find my way out. After six months, I had already extended my lease on my apartment and was considering a further extension. But when there were just two weeks left of the lease, I knew my time in Buenos Aires was up. Now I had to embark on my motorcycle journey. Not that I had given much thought as to 'How.' The only thing I knew was that I wanted to go to Ushuaia on the southern tip of South America. Everything else was open ended.

The physical baggage

I made a long shopping list for my upcoming trip, containing a detailed description of every single item I wanted to buy. I had a clear picture of looks, quality, and what the right price should be.

Although Buenos Aires is a big city, you can't get hold of everything. Ordering goods from abroad is only a theoretical possibility owing to the bureaucracy of the Argentine postal and customs service. Unless you have a dead man's patience and a bank account that matches Bill Gates', it isn't possible to buy consumer goods from online stores abroad. In any case, certainly not at the time I was visiting.

It frustrated me that I couldn't find all the articles I was looking for, in exactly the colour I desired, the brand and at the price I wanted. Instead of lowering my expectations, I chose to manage with what I had brought with me from Denmark, the things I had already bought, and the few things I could get from my list.

On the day of departure, after eight months in Buenos Aires, my preparations for the upcoming trip were as follows:

- intermediate-level Spanish skills with an expert level in slang, tools, and motorcycle parts
- considerable intake of Argentine wine and steak

- purchase of a six-year-old BMW F 650 GS Dakar, which I named 'Señor Dakar,' with side bags, a secondhand helmet and tank bag
- a travel blog where I uploaded the first post (about my time in Buenos Aires) the day before departure.

The comprehensive list of what I chose to take on the trip looked like this:

- the cell phone number of Mariano
- duct tape (purchased in Buenos Aires)
- pink Chanel lip gloss (brought from Denmark)
- white MacBook (borrowed from my dad)
- mobile phone (purchased in Buenos Aires), which turned out to be useless. Ninety-five percent of the time, I was in areas without cell phone coverage. After four months, the cell phone drowned in my inside pocket during a ride through heavy rain
- tent (borrowed from an English rider who had rented a motorcycle from Motocare)
- sleeping bag (borrowed from Pelado)
- inflatable mattress (Christmas present from one of my elder brothers and his wife)
- headlamp with two extra batteries (ditto)
- three T-shirts, two tops and a windbreaker (purchased in Buenos Aires)
- a pair of summer motorcycle trousers (gift from my parents)
- a pair of hiking trousers (bought in Buenos Aires)
- a pair of jeans (brought from Denmark) which had now become too small due to the intake of Argentine wine and steak. I planned to lose those extra pounds as soon as I left Buenos Aires though that didn't happen. Still, I retained the trousers if only as a reminder that my behind had gotten bigger. I gained a few more pounds during the first few months of the trip.

Only when I had trouble squeezing myself into my only pair of motorcycle trousers did I lose weight again

- pink skirt (brought from Denmark)
- summer dress (purchased in Buenos Aires)
- a pair of flip-flops and a pair of sneakers (brought from Denmark)
- granny-style underwear and socks (brought from Denmark)
- small towel (purchased in Buenos Aires)
- the essentials for the toiletry bag, such as toothbrush, toothpaste, shower gel and shampoo
- a pair of hiking boots (purchased in Buenos Aires)
- a motorcycle jacket (borrowed from my Argentine friend Yanina). Unfortunately, the jacket lacked its thermo-lining and was therefore unsuitable for cold weather
- motorcycle back guard (gift from my parents)
- a pair of summer motorcycle gloves (gift from my parents)
- a few spare parts such as a spark plug, clutch cable, brake discs, air and oil filter (purchased in Buenos Aires)
- chain oil (bought in Buenos Aires)
- patch spray for tires (purchased in Buenos Aires)
- pink logbook (notebook) for motorcycle maintenance (purchased in Buenos Aires)
- a significant number of books (purchased in Buenos Aires).

What I failed to bring was:

- detailed map
- GPS
- a personal GPS tracking device
- raingear

- warm clothes
- motorcycle boots
- any idea of what lay ahead.

With this pack, the travel team was set:

Señor Dakar	**Me**
Full name: BMW F 650 GS Dakar	Full name: Annette Vibeke Birkmann
Year: 2000	Year: 1974
Color: White and black	Color: Skin color
Weight (with a full tank): 425 pounds	Weight (with a full tank): 150 pounds
Permitted total weight: 837 pounds	Permitted total weight: 170 pounds (BMI)
Power: 50 hp at 6500 rpm	Power: Unknown
Top speed: 105 miles per hour	Top speed: 6 miles per hour (for a maximum of one hour)
Frame: Tube frame with screwed back frame	Frame: 206 bones
Tire dimension: 90/90 (front) and 130/80 (rear)	Tire dimension: European size 39

On an oppressively hot day in December, with the midday rush hour traffic picking up, Señor Dakar and I left Buenos Aires and were instantly stuck in traffic. I had intended to leave early to avoid both heat and the traffic. Instead, I ended up spending the morning riding around Buenos Aires looking in vain for a more detailed map of Argentina than the one I had purchased at a souvenir shop.

Nevertheless, there was nothing that could dampen the smile on my face as I sat in traffic on my bike while inhaling close to one hundred percent carbon dioxide. I had embarked on the most incredible adventure of my life, and none of the lapses in preparation for the journey could change that.

I headed for Pinamar, a seaside resort on the shore of the Atlantic Ocean, arriving late in the afternoon. Here I rode around for an hour before I found a campsite. It cost 2 dollars per night, and then I could choose a site myself. I chose one that was close to a wreck of an RV, which according to the camping office, was owned by an Italian.

It took no more than two minutes before a man stuck his head out of the pile of junk and asked if he should help me set up the tent. Yes, by all means – I was nervous that setting up the tent would be difficult. We quickly got the tent up and I was relieved to know that it was not rocket science to perform this task. Lawyers also stood a chance.

The Italian had offered me a place in his RV, but I declined politely; I was quite happy with my new house. I had only slept in a tent once before on a visit to the small Danish island of Anholt with a friend – and I was looking forward to my first night in a tent. After setting up the tent, I was invited on a tour of the RV and a cup of tea with the Italian, Carlo, and his Rottweiler, Romelo.

Carlo spoke incessantly for three hours straight, and it was no small thing I got to know. For example, he had a gun and a shotgun. The gun was for personal protection, and the shotgun (which was of the kind that one needs a serious permit to possess in Europe) was to aim and shoot at empty beer cans. The rust covered bucket weighed almost four tons, had six wheels, six beds (of which Carlo and Romelo each occupied one, the remaining four were filled with garbage), a kitchen with a gas burner and oven, toilet and

Ready for take-off, Buenos Aires.

shower and a 100-gallon water tank. The year was vintage – 1978, and the whole glory had cost $8,000.

Carlo was also able to tell me that he was thirty-six years old, had been married twice – first to a Swede (he spoke excellent Swedish) and then to an Argentine. He had left Buenos Aires because he was sliding into decrepitude due to excessive cocaine use.

According to Carlo, the cocaine in Argentina was of good quality. It was delivered in small bags of one and a half grams, which was enough for fifteen lines. Most settled for two lanes at a time; Carlo drove all fifteen lines straight up his nose before noon (which the nose, according to Carlo, doesn't benefit from). Then he started on bag number two, which he had emptied before his future ex-wife came home from work. The bags were ingested with a side order of whiskey, vodka, and the like, while zapping between

Chapter 2

television channels all day long. This went on for six months until he started getting strong palpitations. Then he finally decided to quit. He bought the dog and the RV, subleased his apartment, changed his phone number, and went cold turkey.

Despite the apparent differences between Carlo and me, it was the similarities that struck me. A radical shift, on the run from a life that didn't work with the hope of changing tracks.

After this round of fire banter, my head was sore and I retreated to my tent, where I quickly fell asleep. I slept surprisingly well considering that it was ten years since I had last slept in a tent – my inflatable mini-mattress was comfortable to lie on. However, it got a little damp during the night, but it probably didn't help that I slept with the outside of the sleeping bag inside.

I considered staying another day, but I couldn't resist the temptation to hop on the motorcycle. After breakfast, which Carlo had provided, I packed and loaded the bike, including the books that I had in my backpack, which I tied to the back of the seat (this was before the advent of e-books).

Before I left Buenos Aires, I had made a list of the books I brought with me, nicknamed the Mobile Library. I had taken thirteen books with me and added another eleven on the trip. To distinguish between the books, I had brought with me and those I had collected along the way, I marked the collected ones with an 'o' in a bracket, which stood for 'Snatched or purchased books.'

I also added a section with titles I wanted to collect on the journey: 'Interesting titles that can be picked up.' This list contained a further sixteen titles, including Tolstoy's Anna Karenina – a book that is 800 pages long in most editions. In addition, I had written down the names of four painters that I wanted to read about. As soon as I had read a book, I parted with it, but after a year on a motorcycle, I still carried six or seven books.

First night camping, Pinamar, Argentina.

I was aware that it wasn't ideal lugging around a library on a motorcycle trip, but since the motorcycle carried the load ninety-nine percent of the time, this minor nuisance I was willing to endure. I needed the books that gave me refuge on the journey – a break from the outer, constantly changing reality and the myriad of thoughts and emotional fluctuations that filled my inner self.

I would gladly have carried more books with me, if only I could have left my inner baggage behind. Time and again, it was the mental and emotional baggage that drove me to despair on the journey. Although I first thought it was the changed external reality that overwhelmed me, I later realised that it was my own thoughts and feelings that created the turmoil. Just as my thoughts and feelings had overwhelmed me at home.

To let go

One of the impediments to the freedom of my mind was my reluctance to let go. An example of this occurred a few months later in Brazil when I had to buy a new chain for my bike. In Curitiba in southern Brazil, I visited a large BMW motorcycle dealer and filled up my bags with spare parts. I bought a new oil and air filter, a set of thermal underwear, and a pair of rain trousers (which as it turned out weren't waterproof). The motorcycle chain wasn't in stock. I asked several times, if they were sure they didn't have it, if they had looked everywhere, but each time I got the same answer. Just before I left the store, I asked one last time, and this time I got a 'yes.'

It surprised me that they had suddenly found a chain that fitted, but I didn't think about it further. It wasn't until I was back in Argentina a few weeks later and a mechanic disassembled my motorcycle to put on the new, closed chain that I discovered it was too short. It had cost me 100 bucks, and I was furious – it escaped my memory that they had tried to tell me that they didn't have the chain, but I was obstinate. I called the BMW dealer in Curitiba to complain, but my words fell on deaf ears.

Instead of getting rid of the useless chain, I decided to take it with me (I found a place in the backpack next to the Mobile Library). A few weeks later, I met two Belgian riders, to whom I narrated my experience, without, however, getting any sympathy from them. Instead, they asked me why in the world I was carrying the chain with me. Get rid of it! It only reminds you that you have been screwed. Why would you want to remember that?" Well, that did hurt and so finally, I got rid of the accursed chain.

So how do we deal with all the extra baggage, both mental, emotional, and physical, that we tend to carry around mindlessly?

I would think I have gained enough experience in this field to know what it's all about. I have also read about it in well-meaning self-help books, and over the years I have reminded myself countless times about having to let go.

However, every attempt to let go has been of little success, leaving me with these thoughts and feelings sticking to me like some super glue, following me through my travels across various parts of the planet. Believe me, despite having tried quite hard to let go, it hasn't quite worked.

At this moment yet another such instance springs to mind.

When I met the South American gentleman in Berlin during my divorce, it left an impression that I clung to for years – exactly five to be precise. At the back of my mind, he remained the potential Mr. Perfect. I had resumed contact with him after my first backpacking trip to South America, and over the years we had met a few times. From the beginning he had been completely honest with me writing to me in no uncertain terms that I was not the woman for him.

I'm sure most readers would agree with me that it was a clear hint but it didn't sink in. I knew I had to let go of him and I tried everything. I wrote about him in my diary; I told myself that I shouldn't think about him, that it was wrong of me to be attracted to him, that I treated myself badly by not letting go, and that he was no good. There were times when I refrained from having contact with him, but despite all these efforts to let go, he remained to my mind the right man for me.

What eventually worked was that I stopped trying to let go. Paradoxically, upon doing so, I effortlessly let go of him. After five years, it dawned on me that I might be stuck with him for the rest of my life. I thought I might as well get on with the man I had moved into my head and be honest. The first thing I did was send an email to the man (who had little in common with the man inside my head). I explained that I was reluctant to accept his rejection, and that I had been dishonest and tried to manipulate him.

I didn't care if the truth would make him think badly of me or if he no longer wanted to be in touch with me. I wasn't being honest with him in order to please him or make him like me. I wasn't even being honest in order to let go of him or to achieve anything. I did it in order to create a harmony between what was going on within me and what I was expressing.

After that, the thoughts of him lost their grip. I didn't expressly remind myself that I ought to stop thinking about him. If a fleeting thought of him appeared, I welcomed it instead of fighting it, since I had nothing to hide and no self-image to protect. Over the next six months, all thoughts of him disappeared.

The lesson I learned is that letting go can be extremely easy. It's the mental and emotional bondage and the attempt to maintain what is already gone that is exhausting. When I become aware of the mechanisms that cause the bondage, it's as easy to let go as breathing.

The object of the bondage is irrelevant. The same mechanisms are at play, whether I'm trying to let go of a bad habit like smoking, a fascination for another human being, or a grudge against someone near me. The tricky part – and this is key – is to stop identifying with my thoughts and emotions – both the positive and the negative ones.

After meeting the gentleman in Berlin, I kept replaying the euphoria I had experienced with him in my mind, which served as an antidote to the emotional pain and tumult I had experienced during the divorce. To begin with, this technique seemed to work. The thoughts diverted my attention away from my open wounds and it made me believe that this man was indeed the balm or the solution to my problems.

When the memory of the euphoria lost its soothing effect, it was replaced by negative thoughts about him. Now he was suddenly the cause of all my problems. Thus, it oscillated back and forth for five years.

I had tried to let go of the physical man and the pain of the rejection by mentally suppressing my emotions, so I didn't have to feel them. The misconception that I could avoid the pain by thinking through "why and what had happened" had caused me to get stuck. However, he wasn't physically present in my life except for a few short encounters. It goes without saying that it's unnecessary to let go of something that isn't physically present. What I was really trying to let go of were my thoughts about him. And I did so by entertaining more thoughts about him.

What I had not initially understood was that there is nothing wrong with the thoughts themselves. After all, my thoughts aren't who I am. Though they arise within me and are a part of me, they aren't me. Thoughts change like the weather. They come and go by themselves when I don't hold on to them. It is only when I cling to them (by giving them my full attention and trying to change them), I make them the mainstay of my life getting caught in an endless loop alternating between pleasure and pain, dictated by the positive and negative thoughts that arise within me.

When I finally had enough and was honest with him, it had become more painful to hold on to the idea of him (both the positive and negative sides) than to confront the black hole inside that I had tried to escape through excessive thinking. I was finally willing to accept the thoughts as they were, and fully experience the rejection: to unconditionally experience feelings and sensations in my body, which I had earlier feared would destroy me, if I gave them space. It was this openness to feeling the deep-seated, unarticulated fear of being nothing, which had been my faithful companion for years.

In this openness and direct experience of the pain, I understood that what I had tried to escape from was an illusion. What a joke! What I thought was a snake, turned out to be a rope. It dawned on me that my vulnerability didn't reveal any defect in me or a weak core. Rather, it was only the feeling of vulnerability. By fully feeling the emotions in the body without referring to my thoughts about what they meant or who had caused them, I clearly saw their transience and nothingness. It was like a wave on the ocean that appeared and disappeared. Only when I was willing to fully accept and feel the unpleasant emotions in my body, did the thoughts let go of themselves. This clarity revealed a deep inner peace; a peace that had been hidden amid the emotional and mental tumult.

The experience of this peace and the awareness of its unbroken presence during the movements of emotions and thoughts doesn't mean that I can no longer feel sad, angry, or scared. However, it means that the feelings and thoughts no longer cling to me and define who I am to the same degree. I'm better prepared to stand by them and communicate them to others in a compassionate way, as and when necessary. Consequently, I less often behave in ways that are neither loving towards myself or others. Only this way am I free from the baggage that prevents me from seeing with new eyes.

ARGENTINA

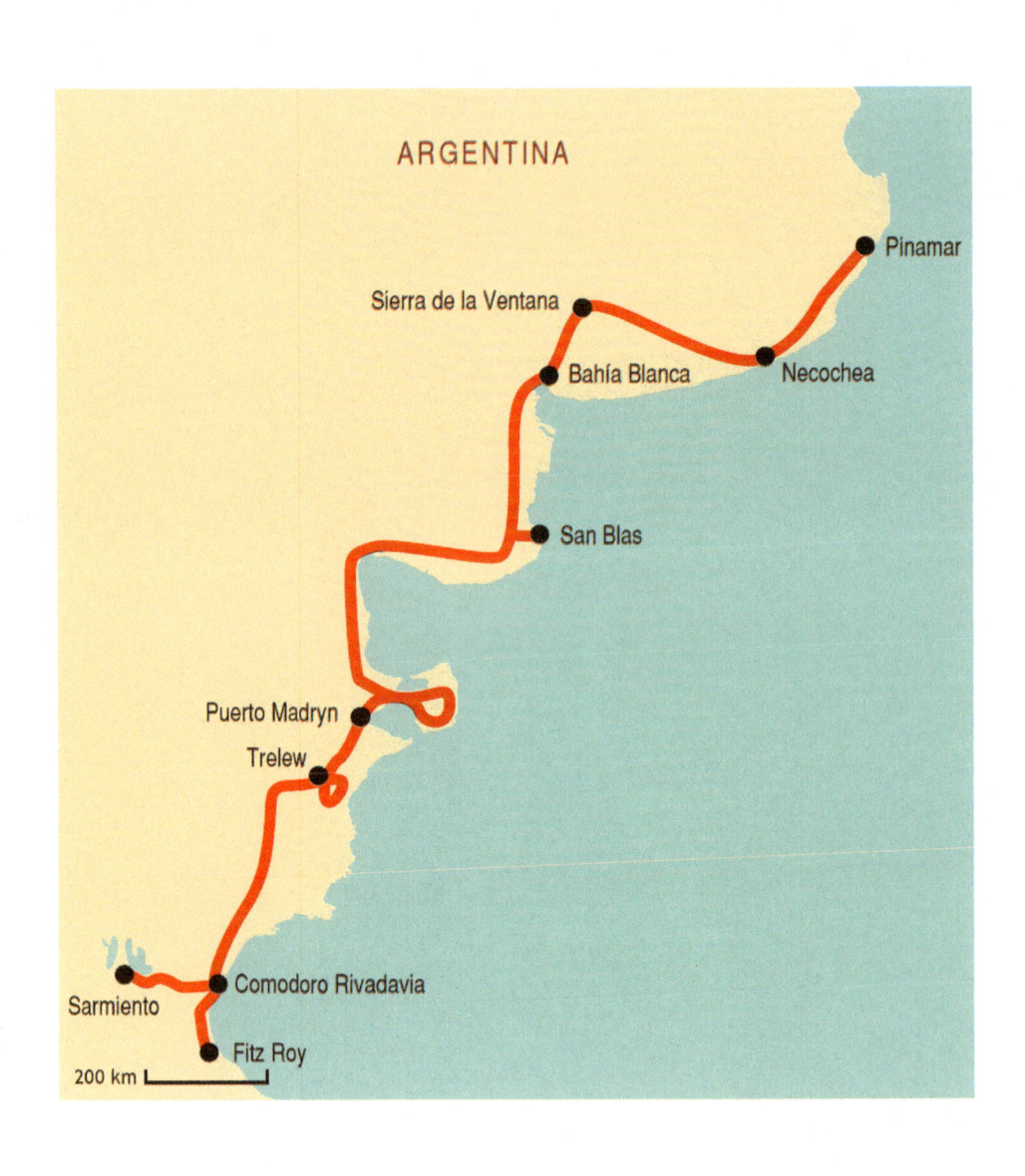

- Pinamar
- Sierra de la Ventana
- Bahía Blanca
- Necochea
- San Blas
- Puerto Madryn
- Trelew
- Sarmiento
- Comodoro Rivadavia
- Fitz Roy

200 km

CHAPTER 3

PLANNING A ROUTE
Listen to Yourself

Trust your instinct to the end, though you can render no reason.

RALPH WALDO EMERSON

When I had said goodbye to Carlo and Romelo, I headed south. It was only now that it occurred to me that I was free to go where I wanted and do as I pleased. I had left behind the inner chaos I had experienced in Buenos Aires and was determined to let my usual longing for acceptance and recognition be the last thing on my mind.

I decided I would not call home during the trip since attention to what was happening at home would deter me from listening to my inner self. Only on Christmas Eve and when I received an email from a friend stating that she had left her long-term partner did I break my principle and call home. I kept in touch with my family and friends via email about once a week, when I was somewhere with an Internet connection. As a rule, I didn't share my worries on the trip, not to disturb them but more so because I wanted to find my own way forward. I kept the correspondence to short updates and to hear news from home. The longer travel descriptions I shared on my travel blog.

From day one, I had decided to keep my route planning to a minimum. I needed to free myself from the goal-setting that I had subjected myself to at home. The only goal now was to ride to the southernmost city in the world, Ushuaia, also called the End of the World. That place had a magical attraction to me – I was in the process of peeling away the superficial layers and there seemed no better spot to do this than at the end of the world.

In addition, I had only two set rules on the journey: not to ride after dark and the second was to avoid deserted paths or roads, where I could risk lying around injured for a long time without being found.

I planned my route one day ahead. When I woke up in the morning, I looked at my map, asked myself where I wanted to go, and hopped on the bike. I thought I would be happy, if I were free to determine every detail of my life, but that was not the case. Instead of experiencing the joy of my newfound freedom, I was overwhelmed by indecision. Just a few days after I left Buenos Aires, it had an almost paralyzing effect on me.

Earlier in life I had based my decisions on whether they would bring me the ultimate happiness upon reaching the goal I had set for myself. No matter what happened along the way, I stuck to my plan. It was the straight path – at least the straightest possible path according to my mind. What I defined as "the ultimate happiness" depended on what I thought would bring me the greatest degree of acceptance and recognition from others.

My new approach to decision-making was to try to sense what felt right in the moment and set the course without fixating on a particular route or goal. Every time I was faced with a decision, I listened to my inner self and gut feeling and waited for an answer. Did something feel comfortable or uncomfortable?

I asked my inner self for advice as to where to go, where to spend the night, whether to camp or stay in a hostel, how many nights I should stay, where to eat and so on. I went from deciding everything with my head, focusing on the future, to decide everything with my body, focussing on the present.

This transition wasn't easy. The many years of top management made it seem strange, almost wrong, to notice what was happening now and decide based on it. I was initially confused and in doubt about even the most minor decisions. During the first month on the road, it was only the magical attraction of the End of the World that guided me. Everything else drowned in inner chaos.

It wasn't the new surroundings or being alone on the motorcycle that made the transition difficult. It was my ingrained habit of being firmly fixated on reaching pre-set goals (to appease the black void) that made it uncomfortable to let my attention rest in the present moment. I experienced so much inner noise from my thoughts and feelings that it felt as though I was riding blindfolded.

Sometimes I sat outside a hostel unable to decide whether to go in or not. Only when I got so tired of myself not being able to feel if it was the right place to spend the night did I turn on the reptilian brain and let it make a choice – just to get out of the stalemate. This meant that at the slightest discomfort I took flight and was on my way.

With such a stressful approach to decision-making, as if every single decision was a matter of life and death, the euphoria of living my dream quickly subsided. I experienced no external dangers, except – of course – the risk of crashing (more on that later). It wasn't so much the fear of a wrong decision that could get me in trouble or even cost me my life. I didn't have that worry at home either. My fear was that of not being true to myself, which was what had got me into trouble repeatedly in the past, both in Buenos Aires and at home.

From Pinamar, I rode 80 miles south and came to Mar del Plata, a city on the Atlantic Ocean with half a million inhabitants. It turned out not to be the right place to spend the night. Thirty miles further on I came to a small seaside resort, which didn't feel right either. Here it had started to rain, but I rode on further, hoping it was only a light shower, but I was wrong.

Out on the Argentine Pampas, where there is practically nothing but grass and cows, I rode through the pouring rain while the lightning cut across through a dark grey sky. I tried to escape the rain, but without success.

I stopped to cover my backpack at a sheltered bus stop and to change my wet trousers and put on my dry motorcycle trousers. As for my newly purchased Goretex hiking boots, the damage was irreparable – at least for the left boot. The boot was dry on the outside, but a lot of water had entered inside. The water had probably filtered down the leg from the wet trousers slipping into the boot.

After a while, the rain subsided, but the dark clouds threatened with more showers, so I had to quickly find a hotel to take refuge. The first town I came across was Quequén, which most of all resembled an abandoned industrial district. I rode on to the next town, Necochea, which was close to Quequén.

Necochea has 90,000 inhabitants with a lovely beach promenade and spreads over what appeared to be an annoyingly large area for a desperate rider looking for a hotel. I was wet to the bone and totally uncomfortable in my soggy clothes and was determined to stay at the first hotel I saw. Camping was ruled out.

After passing three hotels without deciding, I got the help I needed to make my decision. A fresh heavy downpour was about to begin – I had ten seconds to find cover. I checked into the next hotel just in time, before the sky opened unleashing a chaos of lightning, rain, and thunder.

The owner of the hotel – Hotel España – was unexpectedly not of Spanish origin. His name was Christensen, his grandparents were Danish, and he spoke excellent Danish. He said that in Necochea, Christensen was a common name, and the town had a Danish club, a Danish church, and a Danish school.

I was tempted to stay in Necochea to learn more about this little colony far away from the ancient kingdom. However, in the morning when I drew the curtains, I saw the blue sky, and I had no doubt that this day too was to be spent on the motorcycle. I looked at my map and decided to ride west to the smaller Sierra de la Ventana mountain range.

I decided to camp in la Sierra, where three campsites were available. I tried to listen to "the call within" to be guided to the right campsite. But no response was forthcoming. After visiting two of the sites without being certain that I had found the right one, I ended up letting chance prevail and went to the third one.

The campsite looked cozy with a large lawn and plenty of space to pitch a tent with some privacy. I found a vacant space under a tree and started unpacking. The first task was to uncover my feet from the soaked boots. I had wrapped my feet in plastic bags to keep them dry in the wet boots, but it hadn't worked – now my feet were both wet and smelly.

As I was about to uncover my feet from the plastic bags, I spotted two men at the opposite end of the lawn, curiously observing the newly arrived motorcycle rider. And sure enough, when I finished setting up my tent, one of the men gave in to his curiosity and came over to strike up a conversation.

The man and his friend had wondered why my feet had been wrapped in plastic bags – they had assumed that the plastic bags served a higher purpose that could improve my riding technique. They had also remarked on how efficiently I had set up my tent and had agreed that I must have done it a million times. Although they couldn't be farther from the truth, it gave me a boost of self-confidence.

Christmas Eve for one

The following day I rode on towards Patagonia 375 miles further south. After a short stay in an Atlantic village (I will return to that), I arrived in Puerto Madryn, a favorite resort of the rich porteños, as Buenos Aires' inhabitants are called. For twenty minutes, I sat in front of a hostel before I could decide to check in. Christmas Eve was only a few days away and I thought it would be nice to spend Christmas with other travellers.

After two days in "hostel-land," however, it dawned on me that when I couldn't be with my family and friends, I preferred to spend Christmas alone. The others at my hostel were young backpackers, and I sensed that their plans for Christmas Eve were more about drinking than about coziness. Not in the mood for partying, I left Puerto Madryn on the morning of the 24th of December, to find the perfect place to celebrate the holiday alone.

I rode south to the town of Trelew, which turned out to be the first mistake of the day. Though the route was lovely, and the sun was shining, Trelew didn't seem like the right place to celebrate Christmas. I began to doubt my decision to celebrate Christmas alone. Was it a good idea? I was nervous that I would get homesick and upset. If I checked into a hotel now, the decision was made.

I wasn't ready to make the final decision, so I rode to the coast, to the smaller towns of Rawson and Playa Union, but I couldn't get myself to make a stop there either. I ended up returning to Puerto Madryn. At least that would be a more familiar place to celebrate Christmas. It made me feel safe.

On the way back, I made a stop in the town of Gaiman for a late lunch, but all the restaurants were closed. Instead, I found a grassy riverbank, where

I thought I could relax in the sunshine. Just as I was about to lie down, a car with a bunch of loud and drunken thugs parked right next to me. Before they got out of the vehicle, the car stereo's volume control was at a max.

This quickly got me back on the bike. An hour later I was back in Puerto Madryn, riding straight to the campsite on the outskirts of town. This too didn't feel like "the right place" to celebrate Christmas, but I was tired and annoyed with myself for not making a decision. The campsite was large and spacious, and if nothing else, it seemed that I would be able to have peace and quiet.

Most of the sites were empty and that left a sea of choices. Not good. After some time, I chose a spot at a distance from the already occupied sites and started unpacking and setting up my tent.

My plan was that once the tent was up, I would call my family and wish them a Merry Christmas. However, the tent didn't behave the way I wanted it to, and when I finally got it installed, I couldn't get the tent pegs in the hard ground. I asked a couple of young Argentine guys in a nearby tent, if they could help me. They referred me to the camp supervisor, but he wasn't in his office.

It was early in the evening, and if I was going to speak with my family, I had to make the call soon – owing to the time difference it was already late in Denmark. A large sign that read *Teléfono* pointed to the campsite's phone, which in fact had not yet been installed.

Now I was getting really annoyed. Breakfast was the only meal I had eaten, and I was quite hungry after riding 150 miles in crosswinds. I inquired at the campsite administration office if I could get my money back. Yes, that was possible.

However, before I packed up, I had to find a phone box. I rode into town and finally managed to get hold of my family back home. They had enjoyed the great feast of food and gifts, and it was wonderful to talk to them all and hear their happy voices. The homesickness, which I had feared, didn't arise, and after I hung up, it dawned on me that I was exactly where I wanted to be. Well, if I couldn't celebrate Christmas with my family, then so be it.

Despite such indecision, excessive thinking, and a cumbersome tent, I was apparently true to myself and OK without the security and convenience of familiar circumstances. I was able to celebrate Christmas Eve in my own company filled with joy and gratitude. The external circumstances didn't determine how I felt inside.

Thus uplifted, I decided to drink a beer and get some food, which gave me a necessary boost. I headed back to the campsite with renewed determination to make one last attempt to get the tent pegs into the ground. The camp supervisor had returned. He stuck a big hammer into my hand, and I returned to the tent and hammered the pegs till they were firmly planted in the ground.

As I was still hungry, I went to the campsite kiosk to buy food. Not only were the shelves half-empty; the half-edible food that was left didn't appear to have been made from anything that had at any point been alive. Still, all the shops in Puerto Madryn were now closed, so it wasn't as if I had other options.

I ended up buying a Christmas meal, which consisted of a waffle ice cream with chocolate coating and a packet of Soda-Club biscuits with ham flavor. What a feast it was going to be this Christmas Eve! First, I ate the biscuits with artificial ham taste, but just as I was about to dig into the dessert, I dropped the waffle ice cream in the gravel. Nevertheless, there was no turning back. That ice cream had to be eaten – with or without gravel, which in this case was the former. Perhaps not the most exquisite pleasure, but if one imagined that the crunch was croquette, it wasn't bad. The meal was accompanied by lukewarm, day-old water.

My empty stomach was full, and I was in a high mood. I lay down in my sleeping bag and pulled out a sure winner from the Mobile Library: Paul Auster's *Timbuktu*. With this book, I enjoyed myself in the tent this Christmas Eve under the starry sky of Patagonia. When I had only twenty pages left, my eyelids could no longer stay open, and I fell asleep.

After two hours of sleep, I woke up to several surprises: Argentines celebrate Christmas with fireworks. The bombarding fireworks display lasted for a few hours and was replaced by an even worse noise from a Christmas party at a nearby campsite, where foul music was played until eight o'clock in the morning.

Under normal circumstances, I would have thought, "If you can't beat them, join them," but as I was too tired to crawl out of my sleeping bag, I missed both the fireworks and what sounded like a great party.

On Christmas Day I woke up somewhat tired but with a big smile. I was lying in my little tent with my dream motorcycle just a yard away. I ate a good lunch at a restaurant on the beach and returned to Gaiman south of Puerto Madryn. It seemed like a charming little town, where I could spend a relaxing day.

I was staying at a bed and breakfast place called Hostería Dyffryn Gwyrdd, on the main street. Since I knew that I wanted to stay only one night, the decision-making process was much easier.

Ten days later, I was still in town. The day I arrived, I had an attack of acute lower back pain and after a night's sleep in a bed offering the same comfort as a barrel, the pain got worse. I could barely walk and riding a motorcycle was out of the question. I had to stay on whether I wanted to or not.

My involuntary extended stay in Gaiman allowed me to get to know the town better. Although my mobility range was limited, I could quickly conclude that not much was happening in the sluggish town of Gaiman. Most of the 6,000 inhabitants were descendants of Welsh settlers, and the

Christmas greetings from Puerto Madryn, Christmas Day. Patagonia, Argentina.

older generations still spoke Welsh. This explained the strange name of my bed and breakfast.

On my first day in Gaiman, I went for a walk in the rain – it had been oppressively hot and I welcomed the shower. By the banks of Río Chubut, there was a fresh scent of Christmas tree and summer; I noticed the unfamiliar combination. When the rain started, I sought refuge in one of the town's many Welsh teahouses, where I ordered the traditional *té completo*.

When it comes to eating cakes, I'm no amateur and I did my best to fight my way through the desire to splurge, but I had to give up. When I left the teahouse, it was with a belly the size of a tractor tire with the first signs of lower back pain.

For the next nine days, my movements were limited to a walk up and down Main Street. I visited all the town's shops and was able to conclude that the retail in Gaiman could be divided into three categories: antiquated country stores with an assortment of non-edible goods, including fancy women's fashion for those who still stick to the 1950s granny-look; antiquated country stores with a variety of edible goods, specializing in snacks à la biscuits with ham flavor; antiquated country stores with a product range of non-edible goods for vehicles and heavy machinery.

I didn't spend much money in town. My biggest expense was the DVDs I rented at the local video rental store (these were the days before streaming). The selection of films was also marked by the fashion of earlier times; the top sellers appeared to be *Basic Instinct* and *Lethal Weapon*.

In addition to watching movies on my laptop, I started reading Bruce Chatwin's *In Patagonia*. Until now, I had by chance followed Chatwin's route through Patagonia; he also spent some time in Gaiman – probably without a backache.

I spent most of the time in my little room at Hostería Dyffryn Gwyrdd. It was on the first floor with a window facing the main street, but it wasn't the view that made me like the room. Across the street were two smaller, abandoned buildings; one in red brick and one whitewashed, on which was painted RONI in red capital letters.

It was the room itself that gave me a feeling of being at home. There was a bed in a thin frame of dark wood with a white bedspread, a yellow pillow, and a smaller, woven blanket in warm red and brownish shades. Next to the bed stood a round bedside wicker-table with a small white lamp. The walls and curtains were off-white and a wall-to-wall carpet in a neutral gray color lined the floor. It was cozy despite the spartan decor.

After a week of lower back pain, I gave in and had a taxi take me to the local hospital at the end of the main street. From the outside, the hospital looked abandoned, and that impression persisted as I entered the building. A few minutes later, a nurse appeared. She showed me to the doctor's office; it

Near Gaiman, Patagonia, Argentina.

seemed as if they were the only ones present in the hospital. I explained my condition to the doctor, and he quickly sent me off with a handful of pink pills. I had no idea what the pills were, but at this point, I didn't care as long as they worked.

The extended stay in Gaiman didn't bother me. A welcome side effect of my immobilizing back pain was that it had freed me from having to make decisions. Unable to ride a motorcycle, I was forced to stay put.

As the days passed, it became clear that I couldn't continue the journey unless I changed my approach to making decisions. The missing signals from within, the ensuing indecision, and the reptilian brain that forced me to flee at the slightest discomfort made me more than frustrated. I had become unable to commit to even the smallest of things – I was constantly on my way to what might be a better and nicer place.

I promised myself that when I left Gaiman, I would tune in to my body and use my head. If there was no signal from the body, I would make my decisions based on rational thinking without worrying whether it was the right or wrong choice. If the body later gave a clear signal, I could listen to it.

When I woke up on the first day of the year, it was with a feeling that my return to Denmark had suddenly moved closer. There was no more time to waste. On January 2, three days after I had taken the first dose of pink pills, I was back on the road – heading further south.

To feel emotions

If I try to soothe or control unpleasant emotions, I cut myself off from noticing what is happening in the present, thereby preventing me from making the right decisions.

The first stretch of road from Gaiman to Comodoro was straight. There was nothing to see for about 250 miles. During the day the wind picked up, so after the first 125 miles, it was getting hard to stay on the bike. The wind and cold crept under the jacket and up the loins, and my right shoulder began to ache from leaning against the wind. It didn't get any better, when I discovered that my motorcycle trousers were too short (or the shaft of my boots not high enough). It caused the wind to dry out my skin on the shins.

The last 25 miles before Comodoro the landscape changed dramatically. It was like manna – the road wound through a barren and beautiful hilly terrain along the Atlantic Ocean. I was sheltered from the wind by the hillsides, so I could roll snugly away in the early evening sun.

Near Comodoro, Patagonia, Argentina.

Since I wasn't tempted to spend the night in Comodoro, I rode further west towards the town of Sarmiento. This stretch offered 95 miles through oil fields and hilly countryside. I had strong headwinds, but it was preferable to crosswinds. Even though I was beginning to get tired, I enjoyed the last part of the trip. I felt as though I could keep riding and that I was exactly where I needed to be.

I arrived in Sarmiento at nine o'clock on a cold evening, so I didn't want to sleep in my tent. Though my backache was diminishing, there was no reason to tempt fate in a cold, windswept campsite.

I had imagined that Sarmiento looked like Gaiman, but it seemed poorer making me a little insecure. Not because I was afraid that someone would harm me; it was more a sense of vulnerability, of being exposed. I arrived alone on my motorcycle, I was different and didn't know anything about the town. It was most of all a feeling of being far away from home. That's how I had felt every time I arrived at a new place.

Since I had left Buenos Aires, I had to deal with an unknown place almost daily, and the unknown brought my vulnerability to the forefront. I didn't know what was in store for me or whether I could cope with the challenges that lay ahead. Once I had found a place to sleep, I felt a sense of restlessness that was hard to get rid of. It occurred the moment I wasn't engaged in practical chores that diverted my attention from the turmoil inside. At this point, I wasn't aware that the restlessness was just covering up the vulnerability smoldering beneath.

Arriving in Sarmiento was no exception. As soon as I had found a hotel and towed my luggage into my room, the restlessness resurfaced. There was a television in the room, which made me quite happy. I turned it on immediately and zapped from one channel to another to block out the unrest. It didn't work though.

Instead, I found some bread in the tank bag. I ate several pieces of bread followed by a whole bar of chocolate until my stomach was full and the feeling of restlessness subsided. Still, I didn't feel completely calm. I had overeaten, and my body's restlessness was now just replaced with equally negative and judgmental thoughts about myself.

That night I didn't sleep well. When I woke up, I most of all wanted to stay under the duvet, but I forced myself to get up to take a closer look at Sarmiento's sights. Among other things, they offered a small dinosaur park (nothing to write home about) and a museum about the town's history (which was quickly told).

Near Sarmiento, Patagonia, Argentina.

The next morning, I packed the motorcycle and rode back to Comodoro and Route 3, where the first 30 miles meandered through the Patagonian desert landscape – a veritable pleasure. At lunchtime, I stopped in Rada Tilly south of Comodoro and found a good restaurant, where I ate some delicious pasta. When I left the restaurant and got ready to get on the motorcycle again, I had the full attention of the whole restaurant. They had apparently not seen a woman alone on a motorcycle before.

After Rada Tilly, it was back to straight roads and nothingness – and in the middle of nowhere, a minor problem arose. I had carefully studied my map and planned to refuel in the small village of Fitz Roy. Twelve miles before Fitz Roy the yellow petrol lamp lit – also known as the "Oh shit, I need petrol" lamp. However, in Fitz Roy I found only an abandoned petrol station and a small kiosk. Not good. I was 50 miles from the nearest petrol station going back in the direction I came from, and 75 miles to the next. I probably had petrol for a maximum of 30 miles.

At the kiosk, I inquired if I could buy petrol and was told that it was sold out. The owner would pick up more petrol later in the day, which meant I would have to wait five hours, which would probably end up being ten according to Argentine standards. I left the kiosk and sat down in the gravel to lay out a new battle plan. What now? My mind suddenly went completely blank. My head, which was usually teeming with thoughts, was now empty. It hadn't yet sunk in that I was now stranded.

My quiet mind was a lovely new experience. Just to be in that moment without thinking about the next. The sun was shining, and the world seemed problem-free. I felt no pressure to decide or to do anything. There was no unrest or restlessness. Instead, I relaxed and let the sun warm me up.

I can't say how long I sat there – perhaps only for a short while. Suddenly the kiosk owner came up to me and asked me to wait. No problem. I was waiting anyway. A moment later, he returned with one gallon of petrol, which we quickly poured into Dakar. Then I was ready to ride.

Before I left, I decided to lubricate the chain on the motorcycle. When I looked down, I saw my credit card lying on the ground; it had accidentally fallen out of my purse, when I paid for the petrol. I could hardly comprehend my luck.

To listen to oneself

The capacity to listen to oneself is based on the ability to fully feel emotions and sensations in the body while being aware of one's thoughts without identifying with them. This brings about a clarity and equanimity from which right actions spring. This can result in both spontaneously knowing what

Somewhere in Patagonia, Argentina.

the right response in a given situation is or being aware that I need additional information to decide or act in a way that meets the challenge I face.

During the first weeks of the journey, this possibility didn't arise, because I had put my mind to it. Although my indecision was gone for a moment in Fitz Roy, it hadn't permanently disappeared. The consequence of having spent most of my life adapting to others – regardless of how I felt inside – was that it required re-establishing contact with what was going on within me.

When I left Buenos Aires, I thought I could magically change the way I made decisions. Ironically, this expectation was yet another expression of my old way of living: to set too high expectations for myself and not give myself time and space to slowly learn and incorporate a new behavioral pattern.

I had travelled from Denmark because I knew that I had to remove myself from my familiar surroundings (at least for a while) to learn to listen to myself. I knew instinctively that I wasn't strong enough to be true to myself in an environment where people thought and acted in ways from which I wanted to distance myself.

In hindsight, it was clear that my decisions had mainly been guided by my attempt to gain attention and acceptance from my surroundings.

That was, for example, how I ended up studying law. After high school, I didn't know what I wanted to study. I chose law because I thought that I could make good money with a law degree and achieve a certain status. I could prove my worth to others and have a solid foundation for a happy life.

My choice of study also fulfilled another important purpose: It gave me an alibi. If I failed, I could excuse myself by saying that law wasn't what I wanted to do. That I, therefore, had not put all my efforts into it because it didn't matter. If I allowed myself to go after something, I was passionate about and believed in, I was afraid I would feel lost if it didn't work out. So, I stuck to law school, which I considered a safe bet – even if I didn't like it.

Unconsciously, I had carried around a belief that I would be able to compensate for not feeling good enough through high performance and fancy possessions. But no matter what I achieved, I couldn't get rid of this feeling.

In Buenos Aires, as it turned out, I was still in my old pattern of seeking approval from others, but from day one of my trip, I was alone with my motorcycle in unfamiliar landscapes, with no itinerary, guidebooks, or prolonged time with others. I had thus removed myself from my usual benchmarks – external acceptance and attention – without having learned to replace them with approval and attention from myself. That void now turned into indecision.

With the experiences I made on the journey, I created the basis for changing my decision-making process. I certainly made progress, but it was only when I returned to Denmark again that the new pattern began to manifest itself.

I can now see that the precondition for being true to myself - and giving myself the approval and attention, I had sought from others — is to unconditionally feel all emotions that arise – no matter how unpleasant they might be. A feeling of discomfort is not in itself a sign that I'm making the wrong decision. Only when I contain the feeling and I'm no longer driven by the desire to escape the discomfort will I be able to use the insight that the feeling contains to make a decision.

The ability to categorically feel all emotions – even the unpleasant ones – by feeling them in the body cannot be learned over a weekend. And it's certainly not pleasant – distress feels uncomfortable. Nevertheless, the greater the willingness to feel all emotions that arise, the greater the gain will be in the form of inner peace and clarity.

I have gradually discovered what distinguishes the decisions, where I have listened to myself, from those where this isn't the case:

- An apparent lack of common sense. This doesn't mean that the decision should lead to reckless actions or radical changes in one's life, such as quitting your job, selling all your belongings, and travelling to another continent. That the decision seems to be beyond reason is reflected by the fact that I cannot explain, justify, or actually understand why the decision feels right at this moment. The understanding will only come later. This doesn't mean that I don't gather the information I need and clarify any concrete doubts. This was, for example, why I took a "test ride" in Argentina on a rented motorcycle before quitting my job and leaving in earnest.
- The presence of joy. In short, the decision feels good.

- The absence of fear. There is a sense of inner peace and it's easy to act on the decision without the pressure that characterizes impulsive actions. Procrastination of any kind falls away. However, the fear (which manifests itself as doubt – is this right?) may occur later, often just before I take the last step in carrying out the decision. After I quit my job and accepted the job at Motocare, I was clear, but a few months later when I had to buy my plane ticket to Buenos Aires, doubts arose. What distinguishes this doubt from a doubt, I should respond to, is the time gap between the decision itself and the doubt. When the doubt occurs just before I must take the final step to enforce the decision, it's simply a matter of holding on to the first clear insight.
- The decision/insight only concerns me. It never deals with what others should do. Nor does it deal with the specific consequences of the decision. It's free of any intention to show off or to behave to the detriment of others.
- My surroundings support the decision – and if they don't, it doesn't make me doubt my decision. I'm clear about what I want to do and willing to carry out the decision. However, the resistance of others may indicate that there are other ways to carry out the decision or that there is a specific part of the decision that I should reconsider. Not because I am afraid of the disapproval of others, but because they help me become aware of something that I have overlooked.

As a rule, the decision/insight comes when needed and when the time is right – not before. This means that it's useless to obsess over small decisions, such as: at which café should I have lunch today? There is no need for deep insights in these cases, and the few times where there is indeed a good reason to go to a particular place, I have no doubt.

    In some instances (especially those where the decision may lead to significant changes or risks), I do a mental litmus test, where I think through the "worst-case scenario" and make room for the feelings that may arise. If I'm able to feel the emotions and accept the full consequence of my choice, it's a sign that I'm on the right path. For example, I wrote a farewell letter to my family before heading to Buenos Aires, which they were only allowed to open, if I didn't return.

Pt. Cisnes
ARGENTINA
Chile Chico
Fitz Roy
Caleta Tortel
El Chaltén
Pt. San Julián
Pt. Santa Cruz
El Calafate
Río Gallegos
CHILE
Río Grande
Ushuaia
200 km

CHAPTER 4

RIDING TECHNIQUES
Engage Fully

> Most of us have two lives: the life we live, and the unlived life within us. Between the two stands Resistance.
>
> STEVEN PRESSFIELD

Three weeks into the journey, I had gained considerable experience. I'd become better at handling the motorcycle and the feeling of restlessness I'd initially experienced each time I came to a new place now waned away. However, I'd also discovered what often scared me: gravel roads and bad weather because both increased the risk of accidents. In the beginning, my fear was intense, and it almost controlled my life on the road.

That gravel was a real threat, I discovered when I first encountered it in northern Patagonia, four days after I left Buenos Aires. On my map, I had spotted a small dot on the Atlantic coast called San Blas. The map didn't indicate other towns nearby, so I assumed it was an isolated community with few inhabitants. I was curious to find out what it was like in San Blas and decided to pay a visit to this place.

What I hadn't considered was the poor infrastructure that connects an isolated village in South America with the outside world. Few governments spend a fortune building a road to a thinly populated area. That was indeed so for the 129 people who lived in San Blas.

I'd ridden 300 miles on asphalt before I encountered the gravel. I thought the gravel road would only be a few miles long, but when I arrived in San Blas, I realised I had ridden 37 miles on gravel. Along the way, I passed only two cars. It was early in the evening and the thought of crashing and lying injured on the road all night was terrifying. The road was wide and straight, and the gravel was smooth and hard under a shining sun. Exhausted both mentally and physically, I finally arrived. At the time, I didn't know that this would turn out to be one of the best dirt roads on my journey. I stayed in the village for three days before I was ready to head back on the dirt road.

San Blas wasn't the charming village I had hoped. There was a wide and empty gravel road along the beach, a kiosk, and a large shop with everything an angler could desire. The only thing to do in San Blas was fishing, although that didn't interest me much. However, instead of mentally opposing my surroundings, I decided to enjoy the moment.

The silence was soothing. At the Jorge Newbery Hotel, I was the only guest. My room was oblong, with linoleum flooring and five bunk beds covering each wall. At the end of the small room, there was an undersized window with a real estate agent's definition of a sea view.

The day after my arrival, I went down to the harbour, which was a collection of small boats on the beach, meant to be used for fishing. I could always be persuaded to go for a ride in a speedboat, but as I was the only tourist in the village that day, I had to pay for four people to go fishing.

I fell into a conversation with the young, local fishing trip operator, Daniel, and he invited me home to his family. They lived in a small house opposite the boats on the beach. Daniel was born and raised in San Blas, but his wife came from Buenos Aires. I couldn't imagine how it was possible to get used to living here, but there must be something good in San Blas, because the wife's brother, Diego, had also moved here. He was now Daniel's business partner.

I was offered tea while Daniel showed me a video from a fishing trip, where a group of anglers caught a medium-sized shark. It was crazy to watch. To kill the shark, apparently, it's necessary to hit the shark on the head with a club. It didn't tempt me.

When Daniel and Diego instead offered me to join them to lay yarn, I agreed right away. They told me about fishing, and I was allowed to use the fishing rod on board. Despite my poor experience with fishing, the action with the rod turned into twenty-one fish. On the way home, Diego picked up a bunch of oysters and opened one for me. It wasn't yucky as I had thought it would be, but I prefer them with sauce or lemon.

After the fishing trip, I was tired and went to bed early – and slept twelve hours straight. The next morning, I jumped on the bike to see Daniel and Diego, but also this day no one was going out fishing, so instead I spent the day in the sunshine with a book.

The next day, I finally managed to get out to sea with four Argentinian men from a small town near Buenos Aires.

The youngest in the group, Javier, immediately took the lead when he saw my motorcycle: "Honda, eh?" "No, BMW," I replied. "1100" he exclaimed unaffectedly. "No, 650".

This didn't discourage Javier. Scarcely had the boat gained speed, when he got the urge to share his boating experience: "If you have to vomit, remember to vomit over the railing and not in the boat." This wasn't the last comment from Javier, but it didn't bother me. In fact, I found his conversation quite entertaining. He was a good guy at heart who just wanted to connect – I doubted, though, that he caught a lot of birds this way.

The San Blas angling team

    After four hours of fishing, I had caught over twenty fish – including a massive stingray, which we released again. As for the others, I had no idea what they were. Back on shore, my newfound fishing friends invited me over to dinner. All I had to do was show up at 8.30 p.m., where dinner would be ready.

    Well, dinner wasn't exactly ready when I arrived, but the food was worth the wait. The freshly caught fish were delicious and I enjoyed the company. Javier tried – again without success – to talk about motorcycles with me, but by 11 p.m. it was over for him; by then he was too drunk and had to retire. The wine had also impacted the other anglers, so I left the party before it disintegrated. Thirty-seven miles of gravel road awaited me the following morning. They demanded my full attention and hence a sound night's sleep.

A few weeks later, I had reached San Julian, Santa Cruz, where I camped. I arrived just in time to have a hot shower before the bathroom closed at 10 p.m. At the campsite, there were two other motorcycle riders – two guys from Gent in Belgium. They were cooking and asked if I cared to join them. I gladly accepted their offer, and at midnight I could go to my tent with a full stomach. Unfortunately, it didn't help against the night cold. I froze and could barely close my eyes.

Frozen, I got up to a cold sunny day and went on a boat trip to a large penguin colony. Not surprisingly, it was biting cold in the speedboat, but it didn't worry me. I knew that after the boat ride I had to pack my tent and luggage, something which always turned up my body temperature. By two o'clock I was ready to ride further south.

First, I rode 18 miles north along the coast on hard gravel in a deserted landscape. It was beautiful but cold. I then turned south again via Route 3 and made a stop after 75 miles in the small town of Piedra Buena. I found a campsite on the outskirts and asked the owner if it got cold at night. He assured me that it was about 68 degrees °F at night, since Piedra Buena wasn't on the coast, so I checked in and looked forward to a warm night in my miniature house. That didn't exactly happen as it was closer to 38 than 68 degrees °F that night, and I got another night with icy limbs and hardly any sleep.

By seven o'clock I had had enough of freezing in my tent. I got up, packed my tent, and continued in the morning cold on an empty stomach towards Rio Gallegos – the last stop before reaching the border with Chile and the Tierra del Fuego.

The 150-mile stretch from Piedra Buena to Rio Gallegos was the most miserable experience on the trip thus far. The sun was barely up when I headed out. It was cold and the landscape was familiar – Patagonian desert. The worst thing, though, was the brutal crosswind. After half an hour, my right leg

North of Puerto San Julián, Patagonia, Argentina.

was numb. The wind wedged itself into my shoulders and neck, and it took quite an effort just to hold on to Señor Dakar. He also felt the wind – Dakar swallowed an entire tank of petrol after 130 miles instead of the 185 miles that he would typically handle.

After a while, however, something strange happened: I discovered that I no longer felt the harsh conditions. It was as if I slipped into another dimension – wind and cold permeated my body, but I found myself in another place, where I could keep going on and on.

Here in Patagonia's southern part, I came across many more gravel roads, and when I reached the Tierra del Fuego, even the main country road was gravel. Despite the name, the Tierra del Fuego was cold and windy. Allegedly, the misnomer was due to King Charles V of Spain. Captain Magellan had called the land 'Tierra del Humo' (Land of Smoke) when he from his ship saw the smoke from the fire of the Yahgan Indians along the coast. Charles V changed it to 'Tierra del Fuego' (Land of Fire) based on the saying 'no smoke without fire.'

In the Tierra del Fuego, I encountered the first major obstacle on the journey. To get to Ushuaia, you must cross the Chilean part of the Tierra del Fuego. According to Regulation No. 1419 of 10 January 2003, *Régimen de circulación de vehículos en el MERCOSUR*, foreign owners of Argentine registered vehicles may not leave Argentina with their vehicle, unless they have an ID issued in the country of registration – in other words in Argentina. I didn't have the requisite document since I had been staying in Argentina on a tourist visa.

Mariano from Motocare had warned me that crossing the border into Chile in the Tierra del Fuego – as the only place in Argentina – would be close to impossible. I was therefore prepared for the challenge of going to Ushuaia. Upon reviewing the situation, I had three options:

1. Use of exceptional persuasive skills at the border.
2. Find a transport for the motorcycle, either a freight carrier or private person with a larger van or pickup truck.
3. Find a car going to Ushuaia, with minimum two people, at least one of whom had Argentine ID and motorcycle licence, which I could authorize to ride the motorcycle through Chile. This way we could convince the customs that another person was riding my bike, while I got a lift in the car – even though I would be on my bike and the Argentine with a motorcycle licence would stay in the car.

In the city of Rio Gallegos, I filled up the motorcycle with petrol, had a good lunch, and rode the last 45 miles to the border to try out option number 1.

For two hours I tried to convince the customs officials to let me ride through the Tierra del Fuego without Argentine ID. All customs officials on duty that day were women, and I must admit that my Scandinavian charm and my blonde hair failed to impress them. I returned to Rio Gallegos without being one step closer to crossing the border to Chile.

The next day I tried option number 2. In an industrial area, I found a freight company who offered to take my motorcycle to Ushuaia for 160 dollars. Not a price I was prepared to pay until all other options had been tested out. Instead, I tried to find a local who happened to go to Ushuaia in a vehicle with enough room for my motorcycle. I spent a few hours at a major petrol station on the city's outskirts, where I asked every person who made a stop at the petrol station if they could help. Here, too, I reached a dead end.

The following day I took a timeout – I needed to gather strength to try out option 3. At my hotel, I fell into a conversation with a group of construction workers who eagerly wanted to help me find a way to cross the border. It led nowhere, but the support was lovely. I considered leaving the motorcycle behind and jumping on a bus alone, but that idea didn't feel right. I wanted to go to Ushuaia, and it had to be with my faithful companion, Señor Dakar.

When I woke up the following day, I had a distinct feeling that I would soon be on my way to Ushuaia. I couldn't immediately understand why I felt that I would soon be making progress for nothing had changed since I went to bed the evening before. But I felt happy and comfortable, and I took that as an encouraging sign. My gut feeling could be trusted, and I was able to refrain from any attempt to understand and explain my feelings. With renewed energy and keen to try out option 3, I headed back to the petrol station, where I had tested option 2.

Ushuaia, Land of Fire, Argentina.

Here I got chatting with a man who told me that he had just seen a group of motorcycles in the city center. I immediately jumped on the bike and rode towards the center. After circling the streets, I came across a small army of Italian motorcycle riders heading to Ushuaia with their Argentine guides. I explained my situation to them and was immediately invited to join them. One of the guides, Andrés, had both an Argentine ID and a motorcycle licence, and he drove a small van filled with spare parts and provisions for the riders. He offered to help me fill out the customs documents. Although I couldn't immediately see how we would succeed in persuading the tough ladies at the border, I implicitly trusted my gut feeling and joined them.

At the border, which on this day was full of tourists, we filled out the many forms and assured the customs ladies that I wouldn't ride my motorcycle on Chilean soil under any circumstances. An hour later, I turned the throttle with the newly stamped customs papers in my inside pocket and rode through the Tierra del Fuego in the pouring rain with a huge smile reaching up to my ears. I was now on my way to the end of the world.

Operation Customs Fraud was a success. After an overnight stay in the village of Rio Grande, I arrived in Ushuaia – along with my beloved motorcycle – proud to have overcome the first major obstacle of the trip and to have reached my goal.

I spent four relaxing days in the city, where Dakar also got a rest. I only got on the bike once while in Ushuaia – to the end of Route 3, which I had followed on and off since Buenos Aires. Here, a sign informed me that I was precisely 3.063 kilometers (1,903 miles) from Buenos Aires and 17.848 kilometers (11,090 miles) from Alaska.

I looked at the sign. "Yes, why not?" I thought. Why not ride to the US? I wouldn't be able to reach Alaska before winter came, so I decided that I would head for the city of angels, Los Angeles, when I left the end of the world.

My stay in Ushuaia also featured a pub crawl with an English pub owner whom I met at my hostel. Unless one is quite experienced with drinking, I cannot recommend such an excursion. The next day, my hangover manifested itself in a feeling as though my teeth were about to explode. However, that didn't stop me from ascending a smaller mountain, Cerro Martial, which had a view of the Beagle Channel and the Martial Glacier, which now mostly resembled a large snowdrift. However, I couldn't complain about the view.

The next day, with all my teeth intact of course, I was ready for a new outing. I went sailing on the Beagle Channel with a mixed group of Latin Americans. We saw penguins, walruses, sea elephants, strange birds, and a bird egg that looked like a potato. On a small island, our guide lit the grill and offered some excellent asado (Argentine barbecue). Afterwards, we went for a swim – with a dry suit.

It was an enjoyable experience to be at the end of the world, but not the revelation and closure I'd imagined it to be. So, it would take more than a month to peel off the outer layers – I'd reached my only set goal on the journey. Still, I had to admit that my old habit of expecting happiness and salvation when a goal had been reached hadn't left me yet. However, one change had occurred: I fully accepted that this was the case – no matter what goal I achieved. There was nothing to do but return to the gravel roads and continue the journey – also the inner one.

First crash

It took me a while to discover that the riding technique on gravel was quite the opposite to the one used on asphalt. On asphalt, you lean to the same side as the motorcycle's movements, but on gravel, you lean opposite to gain more grip and traction. Until I reached the Tierra del Fuego, the gravel roads I had encountered had been hard and smooth, so here I had gotten away with using the technique from asphalt roads. This, however, didn't work on the gravel roads I was now facing.

When I tried to lean with the bike, it gave me a feeling of being out of control. This neither quelled the fear of a crash nor made me relax on the motorcycle. But if I managed to relax for even a fleeting moment, my body found itself in the correct position and put me back in control.

Shortly after leaving Ushuaia and crossing the border into Chile (this time without problems), what I had feared for weeks happened. I had my first motorcycle crash – on the main dirt road at 30 miles per hour. At the bottom of a hill, a strong gust of wind grabbed me, I lost control, and a few seconds later, I was lying in the gravel.

I must have had a brief blackout because I don't remember the fall itself. Suddenly, I was just lying on the gravel with my left leg under the motorcycle.

The engine was still running, so Señor Dakar was not severely damaged. I felt no pain, so neither was I.

I pulled my left leg towards me, got up and created an overview of the accident site.

Location:

- Location: Tierra del Fuego, Chile
- Road condition: Loose gravel
- Weather forecast: Strong winds and sun. No risk of rain
- Traffic information: No risk of congestion

Motorcycle:

- Left side bag turned into trash
- Contents of left side bag now roadside decoration
- Left handguard: Bent
- Gear shifter: Bent
- The area around the taillight: Bent
- The body: Scratched

Rider:

- Left leg: Bluish
- Stomach: Empty
- Body: Tired and cold
- Head: Carefree

First crash, Land of Fire, Argentina.

I gathered the things from the side bag before the wind blew them away, took a few photos and tried to pick up the motorcycle. It didn't move an inch. I looked at my watch; it was precisely six in the evening, and I had not seen another vehicle for half an hour. How long would it take before the next one passed?

To my great surprise, I was as calm as the bottom of a deep lake. What I'd feared most had just happened. Until this moment, every minute on gravel had been a minute ruled by fear. Now my biggest fear had come true: I had crashed on a deserted country road, my motorcycle was down, and I couldn't get it up. I was in a country, where I wasn't allowed to ride my bike and where you couldn't talk yourself out of trouble with the police.

Still, I didn't have a shadow of worry in my head. I took a bottle of water and some bread from the tank bag, sat on the side of the road, and scouted for a flat patch of land – it might be necessary to pitch my tent for the night. There aren't many vehicles on Patagonian country roads, in fact so few that every time you see another, you flash the high beam to say hello.

Four minutes later a truck came by. I waved it to a halt and an overweight Chilean truck driver stepped out. My motorcycle trousers, which I was afraid would soon walk on their own, were far from being as dirty as the T-shirt he was wearing.

Together we lifted the motorcycle. With a screwdriver, the truck driver removed a stubborn plastic residue from the side bag, which was stuck. Half an hour later my luggage was rearranged, now with the sleeping bag and sleeping pad attached to my backpack, and I was ready to twist the throttle.

I left the remains of the broken side bag by the roadside. It was totally damaged, but if it hadn't taken most of the fall, my left leg would have looked quite different. As a matter of fact, I was relieved to get rid of the side bag. It had hung too close to the exhaust, and the heat had begun to melt the plastic. Now, that problem had vanished away.

Five and a half hours later I was back in Rio Gallegos in Argentina. It was almost midnight, pitch dark, and all the hotels were fully occupied. I didn't understand why so many people wanted to visit Rio Gallegos. In my opinion, there was neither much to see nor do. The most exciting thing about the city seemed to be its location. With its 100,000 inhabitants, it was the largest city near Ushuaia and the many cruise ships to Antarctica. In addition, it was home to a large naval base that was last in action during the Falklands War. The memorials from the war weren't worth a visit; most consisted of sculptures of some soldiers and a sign that read: *Las Malvinas son Argentinas* (the Falkland Islands belong to Argentina).

After my first crash and twelve hours in the saddle, it was no fun to circle the streets of Rio Gallegos at midnight. It took me half an hour to find a hotel with a vacant room. It was one of the most expensive hotels in the city. A single room, including a breakfast buffet, cost 25 dollars, a high price in that part of the world at that time. Somewhat expensive, I thought and continued the midnight hotel hunt. At the next fully booked hotel, I woke up and became aware of the futility of saving 16 dollars, when I was more dead than alive.

I stepped into a, by my standards, spacious and luxurious room and felt as though I had entered heaven. I slept like a log in a big, clean bed. Only the next morning did it dawn on me how lucky I had been in the crash. The exhaustion, both physical and mental, surfaced, and I found myself sitting in bed crying for no apparent reason. I felt vulnerable and weak.

I stayed in the room all day – everything on the other side of the door seemed overwhelming. I couldn't even bring myself to go down to the restaurant to have breakfast. I extended my stay by one more night; the following night everything was booked.

I don't remember what I did in the hotel room during the day and a half that I spent there. I do recall crying and I do recall being scared. I have consulted my travel diary and it revealed nothing. I have noted that I had a crash and intended to find a place, where I could stay three days to rest and read. With the loss of one side bag, I had to downgrade the Mobile Library. I wasn't allowed to get rid of books until they were read – it was against the library rules.

The only thing I wrote about my stay in the hotel room was: "I spent two days in the hotel." The rest of the day's scribbles are a detailed analysis of my failed attempt to let go of the South American man I had met in Berlin and a remark about an urgent need to lose weight.

The crash made me aware of my physical vulnerability – and worse, of mortality. With the challenges that the journey presented, I couldn't consciously contain this anxiety. It was easier to let my mind obsess over more specific topics like the South American man and the desire to lose weight.

After two nights in Rio Gallegos, I reluctantly got on the motorcycle again, but I didn't get far. Before I was out of town, I realised that I wasn't able to ride. On the outskirts of town, I found a hostel close to the road leading out of town.

An elderly lady led me to the rear of the house to a 100 square feet room. There was a bunk bed and three single beds; I was the first in the room and chose the top bed in the corner. It seemed like a unique spot with maximum privacy. Three other travellers arrived during the evening, but I didn't talk to them. I just lay in my corner with my back to the door.

During the night, it dawned on me that my so-called privacy came at a price. The gas stove was turned up to max, the heat rose to the ceiling, and I could barely breathe. I didn't sleep at all. The next morning, I felt as if I had been run over by a truck. My mood was below zero; I had cried during the night again without knowing why.

But I had to leave – another night in this gas chamber wasn't possible. Despite the imminent danger of collapse, I got myself on the motorcycle and rode west.

This day the wind was even stronger than the day I had crashed. Although I limited the speed to 20 miles per hour, the wind repeatedly got hold of me which made it more than difficult to stay on the bike. After 12 miles I gave up. I was stopped at a police roadblock, and I asked a policeman for directions to the nearest hotel. He told me that Hotel Güer Aike was a mile and a half or two down the road. Usually, there are 100 miles of nothing between successive towns in Patagonia, so it almost felt like a miracle that there was a small collection of houses making up the village of Güer Aike. It even had a hotel.

Hotel Güer Aike was a single-story building with a yellow, plastered facade and red tile roof. The building consisted of houses linked together and was surrounded by the Patagonian desert on all sides. The hotel was owned by the couple Carlo and Alicia, and they ran it in a minimalist way, simply because that's how it was done here. For example, there was no landline phone and no cell phone coverage. Internet – what was that?

In my room, which was in the newly renovated part of the hotel (a renovation that Carlo himself carried out, though he was probably around 60), there was a bed – nothing else. A burgundy wall-to-wall carpet covered the floor. In the ceiling sat the room's only source of lighting in the form of several halogen spots. It was cozy enough, though the only thing that wasn't top quality was the mattress, which most of all felt like a giant marshmallow.

I was the only guest in the hotel. For lunch, fifteen seats in the restaurant were reserved for workers in the process of constructing a roundabout nearby. Besides that, it was quiet. If I were to briefly describe Patagonia, this gem of a hotel with its open and helpful owners seems to be a great place to start.

I stayed with Carlo and Alicia for three days, and during my stay, nothing happened. I was hardly outside the house; the rhythm inside suited me. Carlo moved around with a nervous walk. Any conversation or casual encounter started with one of his countless *aah, esta* (ah, like that) as if he had just committed a great magic trick. *Aah esta* was usually followed by a *muy bien* (excellent), which disappeared in a gentle, short laugh. Alicia was a straightforward and robust woman with her heart in the right place. She had a deep and clear voice, which left no doubt as to who was in charge here.

The meals were well cooked and homemade, from pasta to jam. A menu didn't exist; I was given a choice between two or three dishes, although each time – more or less voluntarily – I ended up following Carlos' recommendation. All meals (except breakfast) were accompanied by a large glass of tasty Syrah selected by Carlo.

In the evening, the restaurant was either empty or visited by a few locals and random passersby with a taste for beer. The conversation was limited to a few exchanges, while the television on the bar counter provided an underlying soundtrack that included comedian Sacha Baron Cohen's Ali G dubbed into Spanish.

The dubbing didn't, in my opinion, do any good to the entertainment value of the program. However, at one point I was lucky enough to walk through the restaurant while Star Wars, Episode 6 (the last of the old Star Wars movies) was playing in the original language. I immediately sat down in front of the television at the bar and enjoyed myself immensely, while an elderly Argentine with a handlebar mustache and galoshes poured two liters of beer into this mouth. Soon he was again behind the wheel, putting the pedal to the metal, Argentinean style.

During my stay at Hotel Güer Aike, where I had the feeling of being snuggly wrapped in vast swathes of soft, white cotton wool, I had the opportunity to ruminate over the past thirty-seven days on the motorcycle. I could see that primarily I had been attracted to places

1. which no one bothers to visit,
2. where there are few people and
3. nothing to see or do.

I was also very fond of petrol stations, but they didn't count. It dawned on me that a common feature of these places had been a pronounced tendency for cold and windy weather. I hadn't gone to South America because of the cold and windy weather, so I decided to hasten up, making shorter overnight stays until I reached a warmer climate.

    I bid goodbye to Carlo and Alicia and rode west on Route 40, which was paved until the town of El Calafate. Here I deviated from my newly formed plan and ended up staying four days. El Calafate was a charming little town and I immediately felt comfortable here. Also, I wanted to see the Perito Moreno Glacier, which was nearby.

    I rode around town a bit before I found the campsite. Once the tent was up, I took a shower in the first gross bathing facilities I encountered along the way. The next day the weather was warm and sunny. I got my flip-flops out and I went for a walk in town, looked at souvenir shops and bought an ice cream. I went to an Internet cafe and uploaded my latest scribbles to the blog and wrote a few emails. Back at the tent, I spent the rest of the day lying on the grass reading Dostoevsky's *The Double*. Fabulous reading, but strenuous. I recognized only too well the type of inner struggle that Jacob went through. Very cruel.

    The following day I rode to the Perito Moreno Glacier National Park 50 miles from El Calafate. At this point in time, the glacier was 8 miles long, 2,5 miles wide and 180 feet high, and as I stood in front of it, I had the feeling that it was a living primordial being. Its middle section moved six feet a day, and metaphorically, a thunderclap sounded each time a piece of ice broke off and fell into the lake, Lago Argentina.

    From El Calafate I rode on to El Chaltén, where I again deviated from my new plan. I couldn't resist the temptation of hiking around the beautiful peaks of Mount Cerro Fitz Roy. After a few days, I rode further north – and was back on gravel. It seemed to stretch on forever, and I knew I had to find a way to relax if I was to enjoy the ride. Most of the dirt roads were in excellent condition, but when I came to Patagonia in Chile, for the first time I got the experience of how bad gravel roads could actually be.

Snow by Cerro Fitz Roy, El Chaltén, Patagonia, Argentina.

I had crossed the border into Chile at Paso Roballos, a small border crossing in a mountain pass. I had chosen this crossing to minimize the risk of being rejected by customs officials. From there, I rode south on the main country road in southern Chile, La Carretera Austral. The gravel was loose and deep, boulders were generously strewn across the road, and I encountered holes capable of swallowing a bus. With two thin tires without knobbies, this was certainly no place for an inexperienced rider to travel alone.

The weather wasn't on my side either. Large cloud formations came in over land from the Pacific Ocean and unloaded the accumulated moisture the moment they met the Andes. It was raining and cold and I was terrified at the thought of crashing again.

Several times I was stuck behind a road plowing machine, which left the gravel even looser and deeper, and brought forth a few more that were still hidden to the surface. As the road was too narrow, I couldn't overtake it. Making a stop at the side of the road and waiting wasn't a wise solution either. The condition of the gravel road would anyway be unchanged since no road drums were used here. By waiting in dry weather, there was the added the risk of being caught by a rainstorm. Heavy rain would turn the road into a puddle of mud, and if there was anything I was terrified of (besides all the other things I worried about), it was mud.

The first village I stayed in was called Cochrane. Here I talked to some locals about what was worth visiting in the area. They recommended a ride further south to Caleta Tortel. Although this wasn't part of the plan, my gut feeling told me Tortel was worth another alteration in my plan. There being only one road to Tortel, my return would be along the same way, but since it was no more than 45 miles, I was willing to ride to and fro.

The deserted country road meandered its way along the Río Baker. Occasionally it felt like being in the Amazon jungle, mainly because I wasn't used to having verdure around me. The Argentine part of Patagonia is subject to dry climate with strong westerly winds, but here in Chile I was sheltered behind the Andes in a humid and lush climate. It drizzled throughout my ride to Tortel before the rain stopped.

Caleta Tortel, Patagonia, Chile.

    The only reason I knew I had arrived was a signpost bearing the name of the village. I was in a large parking lot, where I spotted a path in one corner that seemed to lead the way to Tortel. Disassembling the tank bag and backpack, I walked slowly towards Tortel under the weight of the Mobile Library.

    The village was built on rock formations carved by water and every house was connected by a wooden walkway system. There were no ordinary roads. Not a handicap-friendly place or a place for travellers who didn't fancy lugging their baggage around on stairs.

    I chose the hostel that was closest to the parking lot. For a price of 4,000 Chilean pesos — I didn't yet know the exchange rate to US dollars, but when I saw the room, I assumed it wasn't one to one — I got a room reminiscent of a closet with a bed being well above reproach. After unloading my luggage, I went for a walk on the wooden walkways. Twenty minutes later I was at the end of the village. A long bridge led to a small beach, which I decided to explore minutely.

The sky was hidden behind a thick, low-hanging cloud cover, but it was still dry. On the beach, I took a ride on one of two swings and walked along the water. I came to a bush, where I sensed the outline of a rain sodden path. I thought I could probably climb in through the bush without falling into the mud. The further I got into the thicket, the more impassable it became, and the deeper the mud. I couldn't help asking myself why on earth did I venture into this ridiculous thicket, when I might as well walk back via the long bridge.

The trail ended abruptly, leaving me with the option of going back the same way or take a shortcut across the swamp to the bridge. I chose the swamp and headed for the bridge. Thoroughly muddy, I reached the bridge and walked back towards the village. From the bridge, I spotted an eight-year-old boy who had also decided to tackle the swamp. However, he had chosen a different solution. In the wetter part of the swamp, he sat in a large flamingo box, which he steered forward using a stick he bumped against the bottom of the swamp. It looked a lot more fun than the method I chose, but I doubted my weight class was suitable for it. I'd had enough of excursions that day. On returning to my hostel, I fished out Paul Auster's *Country of Last Things*. It seemed appropriate in my present situation.

For the next two weeks, I moved slowly north along La Carretera Austral. It was raining and the bad condition of the dirt road scared me quite a bit. The fear seemed to increase with each passing day. Daily my capacity to endure discomfort on the motorcycle was sorely tried beyond limits.

It was an absurd situation to be in, for I found myself in the most spectacular scenery without being able to enjoy it. The stretch from Caleta Tortel to Chaitén in Chile stands out as one of the most breathtaking roads of the entire journey. Moreover, it offered an experienced motorcyclist a superb

La Carretera Austral, Patagonia, Chile.

riding experience on gravel. But being no veteran rider, I was unable to enjoy these gifts of nature – at least until I came to the village of Puerto Cisnes.

Nothing happened during the three days I spent there, except that the rain finally stopped. When I woke up on the third day, there was no doubt that the taps of heaven would be wide open again, and I considered staying an extra day. But I suddenly knew that I could no longer let the fear of rain and bad weather deter my journey. I had to get rid of it if I were to enjoy life on the road.

I got ready, and just before jumping on the bike, I cast a gaze on the dark grey sky and defiantly cried aloud, "You can rain all you want, and you can give me the worst gravel roads. But no matter what, I'm going, and I shall enjoy the ride to the fullest. It's not up for discussion."

I put the motorcycle in gear and had scarcely left the village when it began to rain. First, there was the 20 miles ride from Puerto Cisnes to La Carretera Austral. Despite the increasing rain, time flew by. It was incredible how an entire hour passed by, as I rode on optimistically sans worries.

I engaged in the ride, followed the bike's movements across the gravel, and twisted the throttle hard. The dirt road presented a superb challenge for high-speed riding with solid gravel with holes and boulders along the way. I barely noticed the rain, even though my pants were drenched, and my boots were getting there too.

It was as if I had switched on a button that changed my world. A change not effected through external circumstances, but rather due to a change within. Instead of being dissuaded by fear, I faced the challenge with the best of efforts putting my entire existence on the line with uncanny confidence. Confidence that I would be okay and would emerge alive and victorious at the end of the day. I became one with my surroundings, and I seemed to be moving effortlessly through the gravel impediments.

Riding techniques

This sudden change in my outlook made me realise that I had unknowingly developed five riding styles during the first three months of the journey:

Coach riding

Description: Passive and laidback riding. The rider is inattentive and has her butt deeply buried in the seat. The rider tends to sit back as if she is sitting on the couch at home.

Use: The rider is tired, in a bad mood, or indolent.

Level of joy (scale from 0-10): Four. Five if the rider has a large butt since most of the rider's energy is concentrated here. Coach riding isn't an unpleasant experience; it's just dull.

La Carretera Austral, Patagonia, Chile.

Resistance riding

Description: Internal resistance to adapt speed to weather and road conditions. The rider believes that if she stubbornly opposes the conditions, they will change for the better.

Application: The rider is in a hurry (even if she isn't on a fixed schedule) and wants the ride to be over and done with.

Joy level: Very close to zero. Glimpses of relaxation can occur (in practice, it's challenging to be in resistance mode one hundred percent of the time). Therefore, this riding style isn't rated at absolute zero.

Panic riding

Description: Stressed, inattentive, and unbalanced riding. The rider experiences pronounced fear. The body is tense, and she feels she is in imminent (imagined) danger. High risk of accidents.

Application: The rider feels like a victim (being tormented by her thoughts in her mind, but she isn't aware at this point that this extreme discomfort is self-inflicted). The rider feels powerless and has no intention of changing her inner state. Her motto: "Why be happy when you can be crappy."

Level of joy: A big zero.

Engaged riding

Description: Active and dynamic riding. The rider is alert, and the body effortlessly follows the movements of the motorcycle. Riding skills are tested at high speeds, but not higher than the rider's inner peace can be maintained.

Application: The rider has complete presence of mind; her riding skills improve.

Level of joy: Two large handfuls.

Flow riding

Description: Active and attentive riding. Ideal speed adapted to road and weather conditions. The rider experiences inner peace and is in a natural sync with her surroundings. The rider stays within her comfort zone and experiences great joy.

Use: The rider is attentive and calm. There is no stress or resistance to the riding conditions.

Level of joy: Ten.

A realistic estimate would suggest that I spent more than 75 percent of the time in Coach and Resistance riding, adding shorter sessions of intense Panic Riding. It probably matches the time I used to oppose events in daily life that were not in accordance with my intentions. This had always been so since I was a child, which was probably why my oldest brother thought I would become the first female general in the Danish army. When something didn't go my way, I opposed it with all my might and strength, and tried to forge ahead anyway. The episode of the bike-chain in Brazil and the rejection by the South American gentleman served as paradigms.

One of the few times in my life where my resistance had been switched off was on my backpacking trip to South America during my divorce. The flight to Houston was delayed by two hours and I lost my connecting flight to Rio de Janeiro. Instead, I got 24 hours in Houston and a visit to the NASA Space Center and Galveston on the Gulf of Mexico in a large, rented SUV, before returning to the airport. It had been a wonderful day which hadn't been part of my plan. Nevertheless, I managed to get to South America, albeit a day later.

My resistance mode had by this time been temporarily disabled by my divorce. I had nothing to lose since anything that could possibly go wrong had indeed gone wrong and hence there was nothing to worry about. I had a feeling of having hit rock bottom. There was only one way forward and that was upwards.

During the motorcycle journey, I became aware of my ingrained habit of opposing unforeseen and undesirable events. It took surprisingly little inattention to switch from Flow or Engaged riding to Coach, Resistance or Panic riding. Having once achieved that, it was almost impossible to change my riding style.

With a few exceptions, I started the day on my motorcycle by getting into Flow Riding. My dream of riding a motorcycle lay hidden for so many years that it wasn't possible to suppress the joy once I sat in the saddle. No matter how sad I was, when I opened my eyes in the morning, the sight of my motorcycle elevated me to a good mood. It still does. But as the day progressed, the stream of thoughts turned my attention away from the joy of riding.

Roughly, my thoughts were fixated upon two things: "Others have treated me wrong" or "I have treated others badly." The conclusion of each of these two streams of thought was almost without exception formulated in one of the following ways: "I need...", "I don't need...", "I want...", "I don't want...", "I should ...", "I shouldn't...", "I can...", and "I can't... "The only variables to fill the blanks were the people and situations it concerned and what was lacking, such as for instance:

"My friend X hasn't written to me for two weeks."
"She doesn't care about me."

"I need to hear from her."

These thoughts arose and were usually followed by new ones trying to adduce proof of the former – in the first case cited: my friend not caring about me. The proof consisted in finding and reliving the feeling from a similar experience to reinforce and confirm the deprivation I was presently experiencing, thereby feeling justified in my complaint.

At the beginning of the journey, I was not conscious of these thought patterns. The only thing I was aware of was the emotional turmoil that followed in their slipstream. Despite travelling through enchanting Latin American landscapes on my dream motorcycle, free of all obligations and with sufficient time and money, I was often unable to enjoy it.

Near Chile Chico, Patagonia, Chile.

It was only after more than ten hours into the day's ride, sitting in the saddle, that peace would finally settle in my head. When I reached a point, where I was more dead than alive, the thoughts let go. When I had run myself completely down, no longer resisting or caught up in thought, those few moments were undoubtedly worthy of retention: every single, even if painful, minute on the bike in the grip of my thinking.

No resistance

Resistance is an unwillingness to be fully present in the moment, that is, to be open and thus be vulnerable to whatever may happen. One way to avoid this vulnerability is to seek refuge in the mind, because it gives one a (false) sense of control and safety.

As the hours on the motorcycle turned into months, I became increasingly aware of how my thoughts affected me. I began to cope with them without pushing myself to the point of being half-dead – both physically and mentally.

The first step was to become aware of the tormenting thoughts. When I believed every thought, I was trapped and left with no choice but to live out and act in response to the train of thoughts as they arose. The moment I became aware of my thoughts, I had a choice between giving them my full attention or throttling their momentum by turning my attention towards what I could observe here and now – my breathing, the sensations that arose in the body, or my sensory impressions and physical environment.

To break the momentum of my thinking, the next step was to give space to both thoughts and emotions without judging them, understanding them, or trying to change them, and they would then let go of me. Freedom from the shackles of thought didn't happen immediately, but upon severing any identification with the thought and staying tuned to the present, with the

View from La Carretera Austral, Patagonia, Chile.

emotions and sensations in my body, I came within the fold of silence amidst the turmoil created by my thoughts. At one point, this resulted in new ways of behaving that hadn't been possible before.

The purpose of becoming aware of the myriad of thoughts wasn't to get rid of them – it's not possible to make thoughts disappear altogether. My attitude had to be open and inclusive so that the stressful train of thoughts could pass through me. The stress I experienced was a wake-up call to get back to the present and be present where life unfolds: right here and now.

Over the years, resistance had become a habit I no longer noticed. It had even sneaked in where there was nothing immediately wrong or out of place.

Only after many months on the motorcycle, for example, did it dawn on me that I didn't like to lean into left curves. It had been an issue since I started riding a motorcycle and it hadn't improved over time.

The first time I became aware of it, was while riding on a winding, paved country road where my aversion to left-hand curves suddenly occurred to me. Strange, I thought. My motorcycle had no preference, so the reluctance had to come from within me. It more than annoyed me. Here I was riding on a beautiful country road made for motorcycle riders and I was unable to enjoy about half of the ride.

I then decided to observe what was happening while negotiating a right curve, where and what it was in it that I enjoyed, in contrast to a left curve.

When I met a right curve, I focussed on where the curve was leading to and let my motorcycle do the rest of the work. I wasn't trying to control the bike or the extent I ought to lean into the curve. I trusted the motorcycle was doing what it had been designed to do and surrendered to the centrifugal force.

In the case of a left curve, before even entering it, I had unwittingly tightened all the muscles in my body, put the brakes on, set my focus on the road in front of the front wheel, and with all my might opposed leaning into the left curve, while following the movement of the motorcycle. Only when I was out of the curve did I relax and enjoy the riding experience again.

I had now become aware of what worked and what didn't. I had observed the difference; all I had to do was apply the riding technique from the right-hand curves to the left-hand ones. How hard could that be?

It turned out to be pretty hard. I experienced a fierce resistance to focusing on the end of the left curve; I felt I lost control of the motorcycle and was close to crashing. But instead, if I managed to stay focused on the end of the left curve and let the motorcycle do the work, I was able to enjoy the riding experience. Although I was scared, it was clear to me that the risk of crashing was significantly lower and that in due time I would be able to enjoy the left curves as much as I enjoyed the right ones.

The key to letting go of the resistance lies in surrendering to the moment, no matter what form it took. When I yielded to the moment, as was the case in Flow Riding and Engaged Riding, I was present. What set these riding styles apart from the other ones was complete surrender, giving each moment everything I had without holding back.

In such moments, the stream of thoughts let go and I became aware of the joy of being. It wasn't the activity of riding a motorcycle as such that caused this effect. It was rather the lack of resistance to the present moment that allowed the inner joy to be experienced and expressed.

Mendoza
Santiago
CHILE
ARGENTINA
Valdivia
San Martín de los Andes
Osorno
Pt. Varas
Bariloche
Castro
Chaitén
Pt. Cisnes
200 km

CHAPTER 5

THE LOW POINT
Be Alone

> Loneliness can be conquered only by those who can bear solitude.
>
> PAUL TILLICH

It was three o'clock in the afternoon, and there were two hours left before departure. I was in the small port town of Chaitén 185 miles north of Puerto Cisnes on La Carretera Austral, where I was waiting for a ferry to Castro on the island of Chiloé. At four o'clock, there was still no sign of the ferry. Two hours later, as it arrived, it looked like a pile of floating junk.

I rode on board, parked the motorcycle on the ferry deck, and went in to find my seat. According to my ticket, I'd been allocated seat 31. A green sign on the wall above the last row of chairs informed me that the two seats to the right of the aisle were seats 31 and 30; my seat was closest to the wall. The distance between the successive rows of chairs seemed to indicate that the chairs were designed for dwarfs.

The crossing took eight hours. Most of the time, seat 30 was empty, but at one point a young Chilean guy sat down on the empty seat and tried to strike up a conversation. I was in no mood to talk, and it wasn't long before he gave up. Instead, I took out Thoreau's *Walden* and tried to read without success. I hadn't slept well for weeks and had difficulty concentrating.

Shortly after, a Chilean teenage boy with Down's syndrome was placed in seat 30. The boy began to stare at me uncontrollably, and I looked back, smiling at him and his companion, a handsome young man. The young man told the boy not to stare at me, and reluctantly the boy looked away. The man put his jacket in the boy's lap and went his way.

No sooner had the young man left, than the boy resumed fixing his gaze at me. It wasn't easy to continue reading, so I looked back at him, and as our eyes met, he turned his head and looked straight ahead. His small eyes were fixed on something further away, while he pretended that he'd never looked at me. Here was innocence in its purest form. I ought to be able to see that. He kept this expression for a while, until he could no longer hold back his giggle.

This scene repeated itself several times, while he kept busy with other things. First, he emptied a bag of chips and a can of Sprite. The empty packaging became the object of much attention. It had a kind of cuteness only marred by a nasty odor of something reminiscent of cheese flavor which arose from the packaging.

The young man presently returned to check on the boy and took the greasy packaging from him. Unlike the boy, the man unfortunately paid no attention to me.

It was nice to be rid of the cheese smell, but the relief lasted only briefly. Apparently, an itch in the boy's crotch had now arisen, which he treated with his right hand under the jacket. Here I gave up reading and went out on deck to breathe in some fresh air.

When I got back to my seat, the itching had subsided, and seat 30 remained peaceful during the rest of the crossing.

Castro, Chiloé, Patagonia, Chile.

At two o'clock at night, we arrived at Castro. My eyes could barely focus, as I was dead tired. Now it was just a matter of quickly finding a hostel, but this was easier said than done. Together with a group of motorists from the ferry, I circled the deserted streets of Castro, alternating between fully booked hotels and hostels. Having no map of the city, and with reduced eyesight, I wasn't sure I could find the campsite on the outskirts of town. I had a hard time already keeping both the motorcycle and me in an upright position.

I stopped at an office of a taxi company, where two women were smoking in a small room with large windows. It was the only house on the long street where there was light. I went in and asked if they could refer me to a hostel with a vacant bed. At that moment, a man came by who turned out to be the husband of one of the women. The couple offered to show me the way to a hostel, and I merely had to follow them. I had no idea where we were going, as it was pitch dark, but that didn't worry me if there was a prospect of being able to lay my tired body in a bed.

After a five-minute drive, we arrived at a hostel. Via the intercom, the owner announced that it was *completo*, but when he appeared at the door and spotted the lone woman and her motorcycle, it suddenly wasn't that *completo* after all. His wife opened a window and stuck her head out and when she also spotted me, she said there was a vacant bed, if I didn't mind sharing a room with a girl from New Zealand. I would verily have settled for a space on the floor, so I took the offer gladly. There was even a resting place for my motorcycle – a nice parking space behind lock and key.

I had arrived in Castro on a festive weekend, but I was too tired to attend the noisy festivities abuzz with people. The very next morning I was awakened by the violent sound of a diesel engine assaulting my ear canal. I would rather hear roosters that crowed, albeit quite early in the morning.

I simply had to get used to being back in town. Not that Castro was a big town, but over the past month, I had grown so accustomed to being alone and so challenged on the dirt roads, that I was overwhelmed by having to relate to other people. I didn't talk to many of the people at my hostel. The girl from New Zealand asked me if I would mind moving to another room, so she could stay with her friends who were arriving the following day. I, of course, didn't mind.

I had my new room to myself, which suited me quite well. I kept to myself and went for long walks in town trying to rid myself of mellowness, but nothing worked. On the contrary, the crowded stalls on the streets, the happy people, and the festivities simply widened the contrast with my morose self-rendering, my bad mood even more evident.

I also had to get used to seeing beggars again. I'd almost forgotten their existence in South America. In the depopulated Patagonia, they are a rare sight, and I hadn't missed them. I had a bad conscience, when I gave them money and equally so, when I gave nothing. When I gave them money, I felt I was doing something for a fellow human, hoping I could sleep well at night. And when I didn't give them money, I had a guilty conscience of having much, as compared to them. A perfect Catch-22 situation.

I decided to let the intention govern. If the intention of giving money was to relieve my own guilt for having so much, compared to them, I would refrain from it and accept the discomfort. When it was possible to buy something from the poor – for example, water, sweets, or handkerchiefs – I bought what I needed or wanted. It solved my dilemma even though the discomfort didn't entirely disappear.

Loneliness

After three days in Castro, I continued my journey north, and a few days later I arrived in the city of Puerto Varas. I stayed at a cheap hostel on the outskirts of town and got a large room with private bathroom and a lake view. The old lady who owned the place was, like many others in this area, of German descent and we spoke a little German together. She was a small, dense lady with a square, fleshy face. At first glance, she resembled a bulldog, but it wasn't long before her helpful and accommodating nature mitigated the first impression.

Puerto Varas could very well have been a town in Switzerland. Here was law and order, good restaurants, fine hotels, and many tourists. Most seemed to be Americans. The town even had a casino. I've never been a gambler, so it wasn't difficult to resist the temptation to go in and sit in front of a money-swallowing machine. Instead, most of my money was spent in the good cafes and restaurants. For the past two months, I hadn't eaten many fresh vegetables and well-prepared meals.

The taste of my first lunch in Puerto Varas – wholemeal pasta with fresh, crispy vegetables, freshly grated parmesan cheese and a large glass of red wine still lingers on my tongue. For dessert, I ordered a large helping of a brownie with vanilla ice cream on the side. I didn't leave as much as a crumb, and when I was through with my luncheon, I waddled out the door.

The next day I tried a new place, where the food was even better, if possible. I got a big sandwich with fresh, homemade bread, lettuce, tomato, avocado, onion, cucumber and "meat" of lentils and cereal. I skipped the wine and drank tasty tap water. The dessert was again brownie with vanilla ice cream (though not of a lavish American size), finishing up with an espresso.

The body seemed to feel good with proper nutrition, though to my surprise, it had no effect on my mood. I walked absent-mindedly around town without actually seeing anything. When I got tired, I went into an Internet café spending several hours in front of the computer, most of the time zapping between various news and gossip sites. I wondered about my urge to read gossip columns online, as I had never done so at home. Now I was suddenly interested in what various celebrities at home and in Hollywood were doing.

I hadn't slept well for weeks. I had no energy and felt uncomfortable in my own body. The discomfort was increased by my stomach's decision to go on vacation and suspend most of its activities. As if this wasn't enough,

Near Puerto Varas, Chile.

I had been bitten by lice or fleas, and my body was covered with tiny, itchy bites. During one of my visits to an Internet café, I googled information on the itchy bites. If it were due to fleas, there was nothing to do. If it was lice – in my case probably bed bugs, since I had spent the night in several places, where the mattress and room hadn't exactly been clean – it would be necessary to wash and tumble-dry all my clothes.

The next morning, my friendly hostess gave me a lift to a laundromat in town, where I dropped off my clothes. It turned out to be bed bugs, for the bites disappeared within the following few days.

I wasn't sad or upset, I was just a little dead inside. Not much seemed to give me joy, and I couldn't understand why. Was it the lack of sleep that bothered me? Was I exhausted from the journey? Was I lonely? Neither music nor emails from home could cheer me up. Earlier they would always lift my mood.

I'd now been on the road for two and a half months, and I had become indifferent to what I saw. I had no idea how to get back on track. I considered going home, but every time the thought appeared, it seemed wrong. I had to keep going. I had a mission to accomplish which was to reconnect with myself and change my life, not merely on the surface, and I alone could do that. I had to make my own experiences; it wasn't enough to read and talk about change. I had to live it, and I sensed that the way forward was to squarely face any adversity.

For the past month, I hadn't had much contact with other people. Would it help if I started spending time with others instead of pretending to be a lone wolf and weirdo all the time? I really wanted to talk to someone, but something was holding me back.

At one point I was sitting in a restaurant, where another tourist was also sitting alone. I considered asking him if he would join me, but before I mustered up my courage to ask him, he had joined a couple at another table. I immediately regretted that I hadn't asked him right away. Still, when another tourist arrived alone a moment later, the same cycle repeated. I sensed that he wanted to sit at my table but said nothing. When I left the restaurant, again I had only spoken to the waiters.

The more time I spent alone, the more I distanced myself from others. I hadn't updated my travel blog in a long time, and I had a hard time even writing emails to my family and friends.

While in Puerto Vares, I received an email from Mariano (whom I hadn't written to in a long time), in which he wrote: "Long time with no news." I was about to cry when I read it. I wasn't in good shape. At that moment it dawned on me that I had become lonely. I had to seek out the company of other people. Not because I wanted to, but to get rid of this loneliness.

With this new goal in mind, I left Puerto Varas. The road north was well paved, which sped up my daily travel distance considerably. What a difference it was riding on asphalt again compared to gravel. To begin with, I missed the raw Patagonian roads, though I'd often cursed them. However, it didn't take long before I became accustomed to the pacifying roads and the modern facilities in urban areas.

The past month I'd been in the middle of nature. Now that I was back in more densely populated areas, I experienced the magnetic pull of the modern and luxurious necessities which I had been deprived of but to which I hadn't given much thought. These material amenities were on the surface highly seductive, as they made life easy and comfortable, but I realised that if I didn't maintain a balance through connecting with something deeper within, I would lose my footing.

Contrary to my intention to seek out other people, I ended up riding to the Pacific Ocean, where I found a campsite near the village of Pucatrihue. The campground being right on the beach, I could fall asleep lulled by the roaring of the waves of the Pacific Ocean crashing and tumbling in over the beach.

It was the last weekend of the season and only one other site was occupied, being pitched by a mother of two girls at the other end of the campsite. The caretaker asked me to pay upfront as he was on his way home and wouldn't return until the next season's opening. Before I got the tent up

At the Pacific Ocean, Pucatrihue, Chile.

he and his wife had already departed.

I spent three days at the beach, walking, reading, gazing across the ocean, and listening to the sound of the waves. I hardly spoke to anyone, although on several occasions, the opportunity did present itself. First, one of the girls from the other tent came up to me and asked if I wanted a cup of tea. Instead of saying yes with alacrity and joining them at their tent, I politely declined saying that I had already had my tea.

Later, both girls came up to me and asked if they could take a photo. It surprised me that they wanted a photo of me with them. They had put on some make-up and looked lovely – unlike me, who hadn't had a shower for days. I must have looked anxious on the pictures they took. I felt quite beyond limits of comfort.

It didn't get better after leaving the campsite. Near the town of Osorno, my motorcycle received a general service by the owner of Motoaventura, Roberto, who rented out motorcycles and organized motorcycle tours. He and his wife Sonia welcomed me with open arms and invited me home for lunch. Though I managed to be talkative, deep inside I felt distant, and I had a hard time enjoying their good company.

What in the world was wrong with me? Why couldn't I just be happy in their company and enjoy it after such a long time of solitude? It dawned on me that it wasn't so because I wasn't grateful for the company. I just wasn't in the right frame of mind to welcome it.

However, I wasn't yet ready to give up trying to be around other people – I had to find a way out of my loneliness. From Osorno, I rode to the tourist town of Pucón at the foot of the volcano Villarrica. Here I would undoubtedly get the opportunity to chat with other people. I had planned to take a small gravel road to Pucón, but after dropping my bike (with the engine off) in a parking lot due to fatigue, I took the highway.

Pucón turned out to be a lovely town and my hostel had a restaurant that served tasty, vegetarian food. I was given a room with two beds that I had to myself all the four nights I spent there.

The first day I rented a mountain bike. On the trip, I met two American guys with whom I struck up a conversation, and on the way back I gathered the courage to ask if I could join them for dinner. They were more than happy to have dinner with me, and we agreed to meet for a drink first.

Back at my hostel, I suddenly began to doubt if it had been right to ask them. I didn't feel I could cancel, as I was the one who had suggested having dinner together. When we met again, I said that I was tired (which wasn't a lie) and that I only wanted to join them for a drink. They sounded disappointed, which I took as a sign that I probably hadn't been too pushy.

Since they didn't seem to mind my company, I ended up having dinner with them anyway.

The dinner was enjoyable; the Americans were both funny and gifted people. The problem was that I felt I wasn't particularly good company with my loneliness hovering over me like a dark cloud. I had a hard time understanding why they bothered to have dinner with me, which made it hard to be fully present to enjoy their company.

The next day I was up at seven o'clock. I was tired after the 30-mile bike ride the day before, but I still booked a hike to the top of the volcano. The trekking team consisted of two young Australians, two serious German biology students, and a Chilean couple. The weather was perfect for climbing the volcano. The guide kept a calm pace that I could easily follow despite the fatigue. I didn't get to talk much to the others. At the summit I sat staring vacantly without being present. The view was breathtaking, but it was as if I couldn't take it in. I just wanted to get down again and be alone.

No matter how sweet and friendly the people were, whom I talked to, I continued to be pensive and to feel lonely. I realised that there was no point in forcing myself to be with others. It drained me even of the last drop of energy I had, and I decided I would rather be considered a weird loner.

The next day I spent all the time alone. In the morning I washed my clothes, and in the afternoon, I went for a walk. I hadn't planned to go far, but I ended up walking 14 miles. I was bored along the way and my mood had hit rock bottom. Only when I was overwhelmed by fatigue did a change occur. Exhaustion made me giggle and I began to whistle a song called 'At a ball at Santa's' (in Danish: *Til bal i nisseland*). It turned out to be an excellent song for a proper march.

The next day I rode to the village of Puerto Fuy, where I took a ferry over the long, narrow lake Lago Pirihueico to a small border crossing over to Argentina.

By the ferry in Puerto Fuy, Chile.

It was no problem getting my motorcycle across the border. The young customs official asked if my motorcycle was from Denmark, while looking at my Argentine registration certificate in Spanish. I answered yes, and then that was settled.

From the ferry, I rode to the town of San Martin de los Andes and continued after a few days to a village called Villa de Angostura. My mood was unchanged. I had no idea what it would take to get back on track. I took my computer under my arm and went to a restaurant to write in my diary.

DAY 87 – Villa de Angostura

"... I am also so tired that it feels as though I haven't slept for three weeks. Maybe I should give up and go home. Go home, be

unemployed, find a law job and complain about it for the rest of my life that I get to spend alone because I have turned bitter and disdainful of everyone. Ouch, now I'm about to cry, and I'm sitting in a blasted restaurant, where I've eaten a piece of gross apple pie and drunk a bad cup of coffee. I'd better go before something goes completely astray. I wish I had my own room where I could be in complete solitude.

I chose this restaurant because there's wi-fi, but my laptop can't find the web pages I'm trying to access. The connection seems to work, but I'm not on the Internet. That's perhaps for the best. In fact, I don't want to hear from anyone or anything. I just want to be left alone. I no longer want to live a life on a roller coaster. I'm so tired of it that I could throw up over myself in thick beams. It's just wonderful to feel like this. It's just perfect. I'm living my dream and I just feel like throwing up because I'm so tired of my life. Maybe I'm already tired of travelling. I don't fucking care about things I see around me. I really couldn't care fucking less. It's as though my motorcycle trip has become a mere pretence. A cover-up, as it were, to show the outside world, while in truth, behind the scenes, I do nothing. The motorcycle trip has become an excuse to do nothing — akin to the knitting I now bought. I just wish to be alone with a vacant feeling in my head. Everyone around me seem to be strutting about trying to see one thing or another restlessly looking for some new experience. A new way of presenting themselves. Is it much better than being at home and going to work though? Hardly. People are constantly in quest for something new that they never seem to find. Of course, I'm no better myself. My blog is a lie. I don't really want to update it *anymore. About how amazing I feel when I don't feel particularly amazing at all. When I actually don't fucking care a damn about all the experiences I have. I often feel like I'm on the right track, but am I though? Maybe I'm heading down towards a big black hole from which I'll never emerge again? Perhaps I'll end up going crazy, which might be better since I would be unaware of the trouble of living. Then I can just run around in my own crazy world, where I'm the only one who understands what is going on. But isn't that what's already happening – for all of us? We probably don't even understand what is going on in our own little world. We are lonely and frightened and try to hide behind a veil. What would happen if we threw away the mask? If we lived freely? Oh, that would be wonderful. Paradoxically it's so very simple, and yet so difficult for all of us... "*

On the following pages, it says "shut up" in capital letters and exclamation marks ten times. Both in the short version "SHUT UP!!!!!!!!!!!!!!!!!!!!!!!" and in longer versions like "SHUUUUUUUUUUUT UUUUP!". Some "I REFUSE TO GIVE UP!!!!!!!!!! PERIOD!" and twice "HOORAY" also appears ("hooray" because I wouldn't give up on myself).

    I had clearly touched rock bottom. I was furious, because just like at home in Denmark, I felt dissatisfied and unfree. What the hell would it take if not even my journey could change my inner state by one tad? I felt like screaming and shouting in rage.

    I paid the bill, slammed the screen of the laptop and went back to my hostel. Here I met my two roommates, an Argentine girl and a Chilean guy who had just met at a hostel in Bariloche and could not keep their hands off each other. Especially the guy looked disappointed when he saw me. I didn't

Near Bariloche, Patagonia, Argentina.

say anything, but thought he was a fool to be stingy enough not to cough up an additional ten bucks for the third bed, that was now mine.

If there was one thing I wasn't in the mood for (besides everything else that I didn't want), it was being a third wheel in the company of a couple newly in love. Black smoke was probably seeping out of my ears. Not many words were exchanged between us.

Next morning, towards an act of sympathy for the couple, I checked out early, giving them the privacy of a few hours. I couldn't sleep anyway. I packed the motorcycle and rode to a somewhat larger town, Bariloche, 50 miles away. The rage was gone, leaving a sense of spaciousness within, as if an inner pressure had been relieved. I was able to breathe a little deeper.

The first thing I did in Bariloche was go to the hairdresser. I got my hair cut and had it colored to a dark blond – almost light brown. It wasn't because the colour was pretty, or because it suited me – in fact it didn't. But it reminded me of my natural hair color, and that was what mattered. The male hairdresser couldn't fathom why I wished to rid myself of the blonde look, but I didn't care. This was how I looked. If it didn't appeal to the South American men, well, then too bad.

The new spaciousness within did help me to get back on track. A few weeks later I arrived in the town of Mendoza at the foot of the Andes – surrounded by vineyards as far as the eye could see. First task in town was to find a mechanic to fix the leaking coolant on my motorcycle, and to avoid overheating of the engine. The task had to be done right away. On the way to Mendoza, I had mentioned the problem to Mariano in an email. He had immediately sent me the address of a motorcycle shop in Mendoza.

    I parked the motorcycle in front of the workshop and entered the front office. Behind a tidy desk sat a younger, well-dressed man. He looked up, and as our eyes met, I got the feeling that he was struck by lightning. Either because he had never seen such a dirty woman before or because he had fallen in love at first sight. Astonished, I hoped for the latter. My unwashed hair was in permanent "helmet hairstyle," my clothes were more than dirty, and I was dead tired after a long ride on gravel roads. I must have looked awful, but he didn't seem to notice. Before I was on my way out again, he had asked for my phone number and invited me out.

    He called me after work, and we agreed to meet. Before we could arrange a place to meet, the connection was lost. I only managed to tell him the name of the road of my hostel but was cut off before I could say its name. I tried to call him back, but when I couldn't get through, I thought we probably wouldn't meet up.

On the way to Mendoza, Argentina.

    An hour later, Pablo, as his name was, turned up at my hostel. He had inquired at all the hostels on the road, until he found me. I was flattered and was glad that I'd had time to shower. There was a blow-dryer in the bathroom, and for the first time since I left Denmark, I had blow-dried my hair. It made me feel feminine again; I had almost forgotten how it felt after three months on the bike. I also put on some make-up, not to please him – I had the feeling that it wouldn't change anything for Pablo – but because for the first time in a long while, I wanted to do it for myself.

    My first hunch turned out to be true. The moment we had started with our drinks, Pablo told me he had fallen for me the moment he saw me. He thought I was the most beautiful and sweetest woman he had seen in a long time, as I had stood there in his office with helmet-like hair, sporting dirty riding gear.

Near Salinas Grande, Northern Argentina.

    I had absolutely no doubt that he was earnest. It was wonderful to hear, and it was pleasing to feel his attention – because I had done nothing to earn it; he just wanted to give it. What a difference it made, and what a contrast this experience was to the way I used to seek attention and acceptance from others without regard to it being genuine or not. I was suddenly free to enjoy the attention in the present moment, and free to let it go.

I realised that being alone isn't the same as being lonely. Earlier, when I tried to cure my loneliness by surrounding myself with other people, it only intensified the loneliness. I had expected to get from others what I wasn't able to give myself.

    It was only when I began to give myself the attention I had sought from others — to take care of myself, listen to myself, and give room to the difficult thoughts and feelings — that the loneliness disappeared. I didn't have to adapt to people around me to get attention. I could give it to myself, and if others gave it to me too, it was definitely a bonus.

Porto Alegre
BRAZIL
Córdoba
Pelotas
Mendoza
Rosario
URUGUAY
ARGENTINA
Buenos Aires
Montevideo
200 km

CHAPTER 6

PROTECTION
Be Disarming

Defense is the first act of war.

BYRON KATIE

After a week in Mendoza, I rode back to Buenos Aires. I had four cardboard boxes with my personal belongings stored at Motocare. Mariano had offered to send it home to Denmark, but I wanted to go back and take care of it myself.

The trip to Buenos Aires could be done in two days but ended up taking five. Half an hour after I left Mendoza, it had started to rain heavily. The landscape was dull and the deep tracks in the road formed by heavy trucks were filled with water. It certainly didn't make the riding less dangerous, but still, time nevertheless flew by. It rained until I reached the small town of Mina Clavero in the province of Córdoba. Here I found a bed and breakfast place, completely drenched to the bones.

As a result, I was in bed for the next couple of days with a fever and a sore throat. When I recovered, I rode on through the small mountain range around the city of Córdoba, which I had passed a year and a half earlier on the rented

Near Córdoba, Argentina.

Honda from Motocare. I barely recognized the area. It was as if I didn't have much in common with the woman who had been here before.

325 miles before Buenos Aires, I was waved to a halt by a distressed motorcycle rider. Ricardo, a man in his fifties with a new Honda 250 XR, had run out of petrol and asked if I could help. I was glad to oblige, having received help from many people, mostly strangers these last four months on the road. Here I finally had the opportunity to return something back. However, I had neither an extra can of petrol nor enough petrol in my tank to be able to share. Instead, we tried a towing game.

Ricardo first tied a rope to my motorcycle, which he held on to with his left hand. I put my bike in gear, and a moment later I heard him shout *para, para* – stop, stop. He wasn't wearing a glove, and the rope was about to turn his hand into something that looked like fish bait.

Instead, he suggested tying the rope to his motorcycle, but that was too dangerous, and I had to refuse. We, therefore, tried again with the hand-held technique. Ricardo had found a brown winter glove that could protect his swollen hand and had replaced the rope with a long elastic band, which he tied to my motorcycle. The result was that he, like a yoyo, shot back and forth behind me. After 30 seconds he was down again and about to drag me along in his fall. I announced that the towing game was over and rode off to get petrol for him.

After 117 days on the road, I returned to Buenos Aires. As I approached the city on a broad six-lane highway, I experienced butterflies in my stomach. I was excited to find out what it would feel like to be back and looked forward to meeting the boys again at Motocare and spending some time in familiar surroundings. I rode straight to the workshop, and it was nothing short of wonderful to see them again. They hadn't changed a bit, of course.

In Buenos Aires, I stayed with some friends of mine – a Danish couple who had arrived in Buenos Aires two months before I had embarked on my journey. I had my four boxes sent back to Denmark, and a week later I said goodbye to my former colleagues at Motocare one last time. It wasn't easy to bid adieu. They had been my Argentine family while I had lived in Buenos Aires, and on the trip, Mariano had been merely a phone call or an email away. I knew it would be a long time before I saw them again.

When I put the motorcycle in gear late in the afternoon, they were all standing in the street looking at me until I vanished from sight. The sky above me had turned pitch black, and I could see a lightning streak rip through the dark sky behind me. At sunset to the north, the sky was blue, and as I rode out of Buenos Aires in the evening traffic, I felt like my journey back home had just begun.

Goodbye to Motocare and Buenos Aires - again.

During the first part of the journey, my focus had been on peeling off the outer layers to reconnect with myself. I had distanced myself from all familiar surroundings and people and was alone. Daily I felt naked and vulnerable. When loneliness hit me in southern Chile, I came in touch with an inner strength I didn't know I possessed. A strength to be there for myself and to get through hard times. That strength gave me the courage to return home with the conviction that even at home, I would continue to be true to myself and make the right decisions.

After riding 112 miles, I arrived in the dark in the city of San Pedro, without as much as a drop of rain hitting me. Here I checked into the best hotel in town with a swimming pool and spa. I had to celebrate my homeward journey and wanted to indulge myself after saying goodbye to the boys. I stayed two nights in San Pedro. I ordered room service, got massages and reflexology, and went for long walks in the sunshine.

Next stop was Rosario at Río Paraná. Rosario is located 185 miles northwest of Buenos Aires and is the third-largest city in Argentina. It is often described as the perfect Argentine city, and I could see why this is so. The pace of the city was slower than in Buenos Aires, and a relaxed and unpretentious atmosphere prevailed. People were slightly more corpulent as opposed to the female porteños (who considered being ultra skinny fashionable). The people here were less fancy dressed than in Buenos Aires. In Rosario, I fitted in well.

My hostel was almost empty, the only other person I shared the dorm with being a young Israeli girl. When she heard I was thirty-two years old, she said it was better to travel late than never. She evidently perceived me as old as the bog people, and that amused me.

From Rosario, I went to Uruguay, where I crossed the border without any difficulty, despite the MERCOSUR, the South American Customs and Trade Union, requiring Argentine ID to bring a vehicle out of Argentina. The score between us was now 1-4 in my favor.

I had been to Uruguay twice while living in Buenos Aires. Once to renew my tourist visa to Argentina and once with a childhood friend visiting Buenos Aires before setting off. She was on the back of the motorcycle and had been a great help at the border in persuading the customs officials to let us leave Argentina. It took us 40 minutes as two women from Denmark on a motorcycle was still too rare a sight for the customs.

I only stayed in Uruguay for four days. The landscape reminded me of my native Danish land. Flat and monotonous. However, I liked the capital, Montevideo, with its long beach promenades facing Río de la Plata, in contrast to Buenos Aires which was built with its back to the river.

Near Montevideo, Uruguay.

After a night in Punta del Este, a seaside resort on the Atlantic Ocean, popular with rich *porteños*, I crossed the border into Brazil at the town of Chuy, 210 miles northeast of Montevideo. I had been warned several times against going to Brazil, especially by the Brazilians I had met. They didn't seem to feel safe even in their home country, but I now trusted my gut feeling, firmly making up my mind that I was going to Brazil.

In Buenos Aires, I had met several Brazilians at my language school, and they had been a cheerful bunch. Even a Brazilian law professor, despite his dusty appearance behind an old-fashioned pair of golden glasses, had a more colorful personality than most. Brazilians seem to have a joy in life quite unlike the way of life in Protestant and well-organized Northern Europe. In Northern Europe, the prevailing lifestyle provides for a stable economy and an absence of corruption and widespread poverty. Though I don't want to exchange that for one big party, I truly believe that Scandinavians would do well to learn a few tips from the Brazilians on how to enjoy life. Now I wanted to go to Brazil simply because I felt like it!

Even though I had been to Brazil three years earlier when backpacking through South America, I felt as though it was my first visit in the country. I was curious to find out why the joie de vivre was so prevalent among Brazilians.

Based on a motto that you are what you eat, I went on an exploration tour in a large supermarket to learn more about Brazilian foods and victuals. Here I noticed they consumed large amounts of alcohol and spirits. Cleaning products were used diligently (there was an impressive selection of toilet cleaners) and bread and beans formed a significant part of their meals. The Brazilians were crazy about cheap, exotic, and fresh fruits many of which I had never seen before.

Here in the southern part of the country, where many Brazilians were of German descent, I got the impression that life played itself out under more orderly conditions than in Argentina. I saw fewer life-threatening piles of junk on wheels on the roads, generally people didn't overtake at double-drawn lines (many even signaled when overtaking, which was a rare sight in Argentina), and people were more considerate in traffic. The only the rule that was consistently violated was the speed limit. In the matter of speeding, the Brazilians could undoubtedly keep up with the Argentines.

Between the cities of Rio Grande do Sul and Pelotas, the road was filled with trucks. I saw almost nothing else. After the Pelotas, the heavy traffic thinned out and was replaced by heavy rain at Porto Alegre. I paused at a bus stop to put on the new rain trousers that I had bought in Buenos Aires. Moreover, I put plastic bags around my feet to prevent the rain from seeping into my boots.

But neither my new rain trousers nor the plastic bags could keep the water out. The rain intensified and water seeped in through the internal seams of my thighs, quickly spreading to my butt. Again, I was soaked from the hip down. And I had a pool of water in each boot. If I were to make a list of the five most significant disadvantages of riding in hard rain, it would look like this:

1. To discover that one's newly purchased rain trousers aren't rainproof.
2. That the rain filters uninhibitedly into one's boots. The result is that an entire Sunday newspaper is needed to absorb the rainwater which usually takes two days.
3. That you happen to open the visor, so the water runs into the helmet. When you close it again, it fogs up completely, so you can't see a thing. This also applies even if you have cleaned the visor with the excellent anti-fog product – dishwashing detergent.
4. That one's nose runs. Due to bullet 3, one is often forced to let it run as it pleases.
5. Riding on corrugated roads (which have often developed into deep holes – a widespread phenomenon in South America), where significant amounts of water have accumulated. The effect is wetter feet and an increased risk of aquaplaning (and thus a crash).

But would I swap with the drivers with dry feet who whizzed past me with coffee in their hand and music in their ears? Rather not. Despite the lack of comfort, being vulnerable in traffic and the sometimes-harsh embrace of Mother Nature, I had no doubt that I preferred to travel through the South American continent on two wheels.

All you need – on the way to La Paz, Bolivia.

Feeling safe

In contrast with my life on the road, the external circumstances of my life in Denmark had been extremely comfortable. Materially, I lacked nothing, and logically that should have given me a sense of freedom and safety. The result, however, was quite the opposite: I felt weighed down by my many possessions, even though I was tirelessly looking for more.

My motorcycle journey was a break from my habit of seeking safety and security in the material world. On the motorcycle, there was a practical limit to my luggage, but that turned out to be a challenge that was easy to handle. On the road, I never missed my things or clothes at home. Instead, I experienced an unfamiliar joy and appreciation for the few things I had brought along. I rarely felt like buying anything. It was liberating to experience how much time it freed up, when I got to a major city and not having to trudge around shops.

As weeks turned into months, the insecurity I experienced each time I arrived at a new place became less dominant. After the low point in southern Chile, I had also overcome the loneliness. I was now able to find far more comfort with myself.

But in one aspect, a deep insecurity remained: My inability to keep warm. It gave me a sense of being unsafe that I was often cold.

It had been a problem since the beginning of the journey. My motorcycle clothing was meant for the summer months. My motorcycle jacket lacked a thermal lining. My rain gear wasn't waterproof, and my sleeping bag was of an older model and not particularly warm.

With this gear, it was no wonder that I froze, when it was snowing in the Andes in southern Argentina, but strangely, I also felt cold and uncomfortable when it was 60 °F and sunny. I spent only one warm night in my tent – in la Sierra de la Ventana in the province of Buenos Aires. It was midsummer and about 77 °F at night. When I woke up in the morning, still lying in my sleeping bag, the sun had converted my tent into a hot oven but not yet uncomfortable.

I often remembered that warm night, as the number of sleepless nights increased due to my inability to keep warm. Proportionately, my frustration grew. The thing was – it wasn't that cold. On the first part of the trip, the temperature during the day in most places fluctuated between 50 °F and 60 °F, and at night it dipped to between 32°F and 41°F. It seemed unnatural that I froze as much as I did. Even when I reached Brazil, there were days when I struggled to keep warm. Though it was the beginning of the Brazilian winter, it still felt extraordinary.

For as long as I can remember, I've had a hard time keeping warm. Not even the warmest clothes helped me. Maybe I was just built that way? But when I read that Thoreau had also been preoccupied with this subject when he wrote Walden a 150 years ago, I thought I probably wasn't a unique case. He wrote:

> "By proper Shelter and Clothing, we legitimately retain our own internal heat; but with an excess of these, or of Fuel, that is, with an external heat greater than our own internal, may not cookery properly be said to begin? Darwin, the naturalist, says of the inhabitants of Tierra del Fuego, that while his own party, who were well clothed and sitting close to a fire, were far from too warm, these naked savages, who were farther off, were observed, to his great surprise "to be streaming with perspiration at undergoing such a roasting.""

– and continued:

> "Most of the luxuries, and many of the so-called comforts of life, are not only not indispensable, but positive hindrances to the elevation of mankind."

Maybe this was going a step too far for my liking. I had a hard time believing that the so-called comforts of life in and by themselves could form an active barrier to anything.

It is a well-known fact that the ability to keep warm is necessary for the survival of every human being. If the body temperature drops by even a few degrees, it can result in adverse and even fatal consequences. If, on the other hand, the body remains warm enough, there is no immediate threat to health or life. For me, this was precisely what my sensitivity to cold entailed of wanting to feel safe on an existential level.

It seems to me that it isn't comforts of life, to use Thoreau's words, that are hindrances to safety, but my attempt to base my sense of safety – my ability to stay warm – almost exclusively on something outside of myself.

For most of my life, I'd tried to build a sense of safety through my external life circumstances – through education, possessions, achievements, and marriage. Nothing helped for, once these external conditions were in place, the fear of losing them inexorably followed. Living my dream of riding a motorcycle and traveling through South America didn't work either. The journey would end at some point, and therefore the insecurity would likewise return.

To be disarming

A deep-seated sense of safety can't be found by adding anything. But is it at all possible to base one's feeling of safety on something that cannot be lost?

When I look back on my motorcycle trip, there was always one way I felt safe: When I was yielding to my surroundings – to the moment as it was. No matter what happened, the best protection was to be disarming and open. Because if there was nothing I was trying to protect, what would I be afraid of losing?

An example would be when I rode into Peru a few months after my stay in Brazil. A general strike had closed the roads on the Peruvian plateau, El Alto. The road from the Bolivian border town of Copacabana to Cuzco in Peru was blocked with stones, debris, bonfires, and a blanket of broken glass. People were in the streets and the atmosphere was tense. Children threw rocks at me, and several people shouted *gringa* (slang for a female foreigner in Latin America). Riots and street fights between the army and the protesters made the roads and every town I rode through look like a war zone.

General strike in Peru, near the Bolivian border.

It took me three days to ride the 250 miles from Copacabana to Cusco. The first 90 miles from Copacabana to Juliaca took a day. Late in the afternoon, and with the help of two young men I'd met on the outskirts of town, I found a cheap hotel in the center of town. The following day, the riots flared up again and the gate to the hotel was locked. No one was allowed to leave, and from within the hotel restaurant I could watch the fights outside the gate on television. Five protesters were killed and many more wounded.

After two days behind locked doors, I rode further north. People had begun to clean up after the riots; most of the large boulders had been removed, but in many places shards of glass were still scattered across the road. The atmosphere was, however, less intense, people were calmer, although smaller demonstrations continued to some extent.

Twice I was stopped on the road by a crowd of protesters. The first consisted of about 100 people walking towards me and blocking the way forward. It wasn't possible to pass them, so I stopped at the side of the road. When the crowd reached me, I sat quietly on my motorcycle and let them pass. Several protesters pushed my bike so that it rocked up and down while shouting *gringa*.

The second crowd was smaller and not nearly as agitated. Two men with a bucket of red paint asked if they could write something on my motorcycle. I said they were allowed to write on my windscreen. Ten minutes later I continued the ride to Cuzco with "Viva SUTEP" (SUTEP is the teachers' professional organization in Peru) on the screen.

I hadn't been scared while surrounded by the protesters. When I arrived in Cuzco, I was tired – it had been a stressful experience, but I hadn't felt unsafe as they passed me or afraid that someone would hurt me. When I was stopped by the first crowd of protesters, the thought arose that if only one person shouts "Let's get her," then I would be toast. But instead of thinking more about what might happen in that case, I let the thought pass, paid close attention to the crowd, and relaxed. I had no chance against them, but I was no threat either. At most, I could be considered a nuisance.

I had no idea how to behave in this unfamiliar situation. I left it as it was. I didn't try to do anything. I stayed where I was, as I was, and let the protesters pass. And most importantly: I refrained from opposing the situation mentally. And at that moment, it dawned on me that there was a world of difference between being confronted with "100 protesters" and "100 protesters who want to hurt me". The first situation is to face reality. The second is to be consumed by a thought that has nothing to do with reality.

By behaving disarmingly, that is, mentally refraining from resisting stressful encounters with other people, I was able to avoid confrontations and

Between Cusco and Nasca, Peru.

problems with others. Although, as a female cycle rider I always stood out from the crowd, I never felt threatened nor was I ever afraid of being harmed.

Another example of being disarming occurred in Colombia when I was crossing the river Río Magdalena. While I was waiting for a small ferry, ten men gathered around my motorcycle and me. I was the only woman and foreigner, but I felt no fear and experienced only kind curiosity from the men surrounding me. A young man asked if he could see my blue eyes behind the sunglasses. I lifted my glasses, he smiled, and I slid my sunglasses down over my eyes again.

Being disarming didn't mean that I failed to lock my motorcycle, that I didn't hide my money, or that I wasn't able to say "no" to others. Sometimes it is best to turn around and get away as quickly as possible.

To be disarming and open means that I'm more able to clearly sense and perceive what is happening around me, which empowers me to let the right action happen by itself. This means that my actions aren't the result of a mental process solely based on memory but a direct response to what is happening now. If I oppose the present moment as it is, if I tense all muscles and try to protect myself behind a wall, how will I sense what is happening in the present moment and act in a way that meets the immediate challenge?

No two situations are alike. If I behave in the same way, no matter how a challenge takes shape, I won't hit the mark. Being disarming and open has nothing to do with passivity – on the contrary. It means that I'm attentive and relaxed and that it's from this position I take action – if necessary.

PARAGUAY
San Antonio de los Cobres
Salta
Asunción
Formosa
Cd. del Este
Curitiba
Posadas
Resistencia
Florianópolis
ARGENTINA
BRAZIL
Porto Alegre
200 km

CHAPTER 7

PROBLEM-SOLVING
Be Honest

Honesty is the first chapter in the book of wisdom.

THOMAS JEFFERSON

From Porto Alegre, I rode to the town of Tramandaí, where I spent the night. The following day, I rode along a narrow road, partly paved, partly gravel, on the Atlantic coast skirted by miles of white, Brazilian sandy beaches. So exotic was the scene that I couldn't fathom that I was in Brazil on a motorcycle and I in fact felt comfortable. With the sun shining above in a clear sky, Dakar's engine spun smoothly beneath me. I encountered mud several times and got to practice my riding technique. It was the first time I thought riding in mud was a good experience.

In the small village of Armação on the island of Santa Catarina, 250 miles further north, I celebrated my 33rd birthday. I had found a hostel on the beach with a terrace, a hammock, and sea views and woke up on my birthday with a sense of calm. It promised to be a good day.

North of Tramandaí, Brazil.

At breakfast, which consisted of pancakes, fresh fruit and freshly squeezed juice, I told one of the staff members that it was my birthday. Then he disappeared momentarily and reappeared with a green T-shirt that said Brasil in yellow print. Happy birthday, he greeted. What a wonderful gesture. I felt so happy.

Shortly after, a young Brazilian man came up to me and asked if I was the girl on the motorcycle. Yes, that was me. He enquired if he could keep me company. Of course, it was quite a welcome move! He was from São Paulo and was spending this weekend in Armação with some family. Since he spoke fluent English, the conversation ran smoothly. Before I came to Brazil, I had been told that all Brazilians understood Spanish. Reciprocally, however, this was not the case with my Spanish – sometimes I felt that I might as well speak Danish.

We went for a walk on the beach and went swimming. I plunged into the waves with a deep joyful belly laugh. When we got back to the hostel, we said goodbye. He was going back to work the following day. I don't quite remember how I spent the evening of my birthday. My diary is silent on this matter.

Maybe I had already started reading Hermann Hesse's *Steppenwolf*, which I came across on a hostel bookshelf. It was rare that I found books in hostels I wanted to read – crime and chick-lit seemed to be popular genres here, but I still needed support for my inner journey from books that made me reflect and ponder.

Steppenwolf was no exception. I read it cover to cover at one stretch. At the end of the book, the main character, Harry Haller, finds himself in a magical theatre (meant for madmen only; you lose your mind if you enter) after having killed the woman he loves in a fit of jealousy. Here, he is told that it would serve him right if he were condemned to the severest of penalties: to bring the dead woman back to life and marry her. No, I'm not ready for that, it would only be a disaster, Haller replies, to which he is told: "It is time to come to your senses. You are to live and to learn to laugh. You are to learn to listen to the cursed radio music of life and to revere the spirit behind it and to laugh at its distortions. So, there you are. More shall not be asked of you."

I did have a déjà vu of a theme familiar from my own life. I pondered on what would happen, if I got what I desperately wanted and allowed myself to enjoy the banalities of life. That certainly wouldn't work, nor did I deserve that. The thought made me laugh.

After a week in Armação, I packed the motorcycle. In the middle of the afternoon, I left for Curitiba and let a three-lane highway winding through small mountains lead me to the destination of the day. It was six o'clock when I arrived. The sun had just set. Before I left Armação I had booked online a bed in a hostel, but without GPS, or a map of the city it wasn't easy to find my way in a pitch-dark evening. It took me an hour and a half, causing me to break my ground rule of not riding in the dark.

From Curitiba, I rode west to Foz do Iguaçu, where I spent two days. I made a short visit to the waterfalls that I had visited earlier on my backpacking trip to South America and took a tour of the great Itaipú Dam. Nerdy and very exciting. I was the only tourist; the other two on the tour were new employees at the dam. At that time, the Itaipú Dam was the largest hydroelectric dam in the world. It supplied Brazil with 25 percent of the country's energy consumption and Paraguay with 90 percent. Today, there are dams in China that are larger.

The next destination was Paraguay, of which I knew nothing. I hadn't even met other travelers who had been there and who could advise me.

Paraguay covers an area ten times larger than Denmark's and has 6.4 million inhabitants, of which 1.5 million live in the capital Asunción. There are two official languages, Spanish and Guaraní. The only word I learned in Guaraní was "y," which means water and is pronounced like a sound that expresses something disgusting. The landscape was reminiscent of that in Uruguay and therefore also of the Danish. A unique thing about Paraguay was the many boxwood trees by the houses along the country road that had been cut into all sorts of shapes. A very popular leisure activity, as it seemed.

I spent the night in Asunción, where I stayed at the Hotel Plaza in the center. The hotel had no parking, only an atrium courtyard where I was offered parking for my motorcycle. To get to the courtyard, I rode the motorcycle up a small flight of stairs to the hotel's front door and in through the front desk, while the receptionist smiled broadly behind the counter.

I unloaded my things in the room and went out to explore the city on foot. It wasn't that there was much to see. What caught my attention were the many orange trees, karaoke bars where people roared – at seven o'clock

Asunción, Paraguay.

in the evening on Friday nights they were full – and chess-players sitting at long tables in a town square.

A few days later I rode into Argentina again. I still stuck to my decision of making plans for only one day at a time and had set course for the city of

Road assistance near Formosa, Argentina.

Salta 620 miles to the west. I'd visited Salta on my first trip to South America and liked it.

I didn't get far, though. Eighteen miles south of the city of Formosa on the border with Paraguay, the motorcycle's oil lamp shone. I stopped and watched the oil run out. I rode back to a police roadblock I'd just passed, and with the help of the police, I waved a man in a pickup truck to the side, who gave Señor Dakar and me a lift to Formosa on the truck bed.

Alberto, as the man was called, was in his mid-fifties and seemed to be a person with his heart in the right place. He invited me home so I could meet his wife, Teresa.

Teresa was a small, sturdy loquacious woman, with a well-developed ability to take charge. She had prepared lunch for Alberto and invited me to join them. I sensed that I wouldn't get far with a "no, thank you," even though I wasn't hungry.

During lunch, she laid out a plan for me and my motorcycle. I had to leave the motorcycle with them until we had found a mechanic. Once the mechanic had been located, she would take me on a sightseeing tour of Formosa. Not only did she want me to stay for dinner in the evening, she also wanted me to stay through the night. I was their guest, and as such I had to sleep in her and Alberto's bed. They would sleep on the couch in the living room.

I felt somewhat taken aback by this plan. I didn't want to spend the night with them, and certainly not in their bed. I tried to explain this sparingly without directly refusing the invitation – I was afraid of appearing ungrateful for their help. Not until late afternoon did I manage to tell her that I preferred to stay at a hotel. She would hear none of that.

Back in the house after the sightseeing trip, the mechanic that Teresa had contacted came by and picked up the motorcycle. I was tired and most of all wanted to be alone, so I tried again in vain to say that I would rather stay at a hotel. Eventually, I started to cry, and only then did Teresa give up persuading me to stay.

The oil leak turned out to have been caused by a defective *bulbo de presión de aceite*, in English an oil pressure switch. I had an extra secondhand switch in the spare parts compartment of my backpack. In Chile I'd had the switch changed before the oil leak had started and had retained the old switch as a spare.

The mechanic installed the switch, and I called the BMW dealer in Buenos Aires and ordered a new one, which I asked them to send to the bus station in Salta. This way I didn't have to wait for it in Formosa, a town unburdened by attractions. Here foreign tourists were so rare that I was greeted by two questions every time I walked into a store: Where do you come from and what are you doing here?

The next afternoon, the motorcycle was ready. I said goodbye to Teresa and Alberto, thanked them for their help and rode once again towards Salta. Hardly did I reach the police roadblock than the oil lamp lit up again – evidently, my spare switch was also defective. I quickly turned around and immediately called the BMW dealer in Buenos Aires to ask them to send my new oil pressure switch to Formosa instead of Salta. Unfortunately, the contact had already been sent, and what was worse – it was the last one they had in stock, not only in Buenos Aires but throughout Argentina.

I was 620 miles from my spare part and wouldn't be able to reach Salta with a defective oil pressure switch. I was so annoyed with myself for ending up in this situation that I was immediately consumed by a narrow tunnel vision which prevented me from exploring other ways to resolve the issue at hand. To me, there was only one way forward and it was to get hold of the damn switch which was on its way to Salta.

I started by contacting the bus company responsible for the freight. They refused to send the package on to Formosa – I had to pay cash (a total of 6 dollars) for the shipment in Salta before it could be sent on. Then I tried to persuade a bus driver in Formosa to take an envelope with 6 dollars to Salta. But no, he didn't want to be responsible for the money. If he were to bring the envelope, I would have to send it as a package and have a third person pick it up.

Here I started to get tired and talked to Teresa about the problem. I had called her when I was back in Formosa, since she was a woman of action set to resolve the issue. First, she contacted a couple of acquaintances in Salta, who, however, couldn't help. Then she called the police station in town and asked a random officer if he would go to the bus station, pay for and forward the parcel and wait a few days for me to come to Salta and pay him back.

New tires, Formosa, Argentina.

Her eldest son was a police officer near Formosa, and she believed that the Argentine police force were always of service to the citizens.

A more foolish plan probably couldn't exist, I thought. I didn't know much about the Argentine police, though I knew enough to be careful not to trust them. As in Brazil, it wasn't uncommon for police to set up roadblocks and demand money from passers-by for their living necessities or to pay for their excesses of the weekend. Two days later, however, as I stood with my new oil pressure switch in hand, I did revise my view of the Argentine police.

The oil pressure switch was installed and for the third time, I was on my way to Salta. I left late in the afternoon and made a stop for the night in the town of Resistencia, 100 miles south of Formosa. On the outskirts, I caught sight of a sign that read "Hotel Faro." It was already getting dark, so I turned down the long driveway and wondered why someone had placed a red, flashing light at the entrance to the driveway. In front of the main door, I parked the motorcycle, went up the stairs and knocked. A small hatch in the door was opened and a man looked out.

I felt a little uncomfortable, so I asked to see a room before checking in. There were a red lamp and a private parking space hidden by a curtain in front of each room. When he opened the door to the room, the penny dropped. In the glow of yet another red lamp, hardcore porn was playing on the television. The bed was upholstered with a sheet that appeared to be made of thick plastic wrap. I looked at the man and said this wasn't the place for me. He agreed but added I was always welcome back with my boyfriend.

In the center of Resistencia, I found a nice hotel and after a good night's sleep, I was able to continue towards Salta. I rode 550 miles in ten hours. The first 450 miles on Route 16 was straight and I didn't make a single turn.

Tilcara, north of Salta, Argentina.

In addition to staying awake on the motorcycle, the biggest challenge was to avoid colliding with the animals frequently about on the road. Most were large pigs and homeless dogs, but I also crossed ways with a galloping horse. Sixty miles from Salta the animal population thinned out and was replaced by snow in the mountains. I was exhausted and frozen, but there was nowhere to stop – not so much as a shelter in sight. The only way forward was to keep going.

I stayed in Salta for a week, reimbursed the helpful police officer and headed further west to the village of Cachi. Cachi is located on the Pan-American Highway (Route 40, which I knew from Patagonia) at 8,200 feet. It's the road to one of the highest passes you can pass by in or on a motorized vehicle on the South American continent. I had to try this out.

Honesty

Honesty to oneself is simple as a principle. It's about saying yes when you mean yes, and no when you mean no. But that may be easier said than done.

It was 100 miles from Salta to Cachi and it took three hours because I stopped countless times to take pictures. My plan was to ride over the high pass to San Antonio de los Cobres, but the locals I spoke to advised me not to ride alone. It was the beginning of June, so winter had set in, and the tourist season was over. If I had a serious crash, I could be lying around for a while before I was found.

In the town's central square, I met a Dutchman on a tour of South America with a dachshund. He drove a jeep and was willing to accompany me across the pass. Together we set off, me in front on the bike and the Dutchman as a rearguard in the jeep.

It was one of the most scenic stretches on my trip. The barren, raw mountains in golden tones with a deep blue sky in the background were a

Near Cachi, Argentina

breathtaking sight. With the Dutchman in the jeep behind me, I was able to relax and enjoy the ride.

Apart from a river that we crossed several times, there were not too many challenges on the gravel road. The gravel was hard and relatively even. However, at an altitude of 15,000 feet, I had a fall in a sharp, sandy curve. I fell on the right side where only my side bag hung, so I escaped the fall without so much as a bruise. The Dutchman helped me get the motorcycle up and I put my luggage in the jeep. Señor Dakar had lost most of his power in the altitude and so had I.

When we reached the Abra el Acay Pass at an altitude of 16,059 feet, I had altitude sickness. I didn't take many photos, although the view was unsurpassed. I was going down that blasted mountain and it had to be fast. I had a harder time enjoying the ride down than on the way up. "Down" was perhaps a bit of an exaggeration, for San Antonio was at an altitude of 12,500 feet.

Near Cachi, Argentina.

In San Antonio, I experienced first-hand how dishonesty backfires.

We had been on the road for seven hours, when we arrived. I felt terrible; my head felt like it was about to explode, and I was nauseous. After walking around the village for half an hour, we checked into a hotel with a communal kitchen. There was a large and a small room available, and without further thought, I put my things in the large room.

Here the Dutchman protested and suggested that we draw lots as to who should have the bigger room. A silly idea, I thought, but I agreed to it and lost, as I had expected. I could well see the rationale of him having the big room since he had a dog with him.

At the hotel, my altitude sickness worsened and culminated in me throwing up. I told the Dutchman, who didn't have altitude sickness that he would probably have to buy the groceries for dinner on his own. He seemed indignant, which I thought was too much. Still, I shouldn't exaggerate how

Near San Antonio de los Cobres, Argentina.

bad I felt either, I thought. In fact, I felt better after I'd thrown up, so I guessed I could go shopping after all.

The grocery store was just around the corner, so the shopping was quickly done. I had hoped that the Dutchman would offer to cook – but again he offered no help. I was doing all the chopping and also had the pleasure of doing the dishes.

The next morning, we sat at breakfast. The altitude sickness was almost gone, and I had picked up bread at the grocery store and set the table. The Dutchman took out a pile of oranges and began squeezing juice. I figured I would be offered a glass, but he drank it all.

This selfishness was too much for me to endure, which I commented on, and it seemed that he felt guilty. He took out the last orange and began to squeeze it. Offended, I said that now I didn't want the juice at all. He gave

Abra el Acay, over 16,000 feet altitude, Argentina.

up squeezing the last orange, and I finished the job and expected to take a small sip after I had done the dishes.

Instead, he picked up the glass and was about to drink even the last bit of juice. I looked at him in amazement, which made him put the glass down. I admitted that I had been offended which was why I had said no to the last juice. "But that was very stupid," he said. "Just as stupid as when you demonstrated your extreme selfishness," I retorted, drinking the last of the juice.

For the rest of the time, we travelled together, the atmosphere between us was cold. Outwardly, we both put on our best behavior, but my head was filled with thoughts of how ridiculous, thoughtless, and selfish he was.

It wasn't until much later that it dawned on me that these words could equally well be used to describe my own behavior. It was selfish, ridiculous, and thoughtless that I wasn't honest. Selfish to assume I could have the big room when it was he who needed it more to accommodate his dog. Foolish to think he knew how bad I felt when I had altitude sickness. And reckless towards myself for not asking for help with shopping and cooking when I needed it.

I had been dishonest because I didn't want to be a burden. It may sound thoughtful at first, but if I ask myself why I didn't want to be a burden, the answer wasn't so selfless. I didn't want to appear weak, and in trying to appear differently to another human being, I was willing to cross my own boundaries, be dishonest, and even end up being offended.

Another example of this kind of dishonesty happened sometime later, when I met another traveller with whom I fell in love. At one point, he started telling me about one of his ex-girlfriends. I pretended to be interested in hearing about her and even asked some questions to make sure I appeared sincere. I would hate to be perceived as insecure and prudish.

The more he talked about his ex-girlfriend (who according to the man was incredibly beautiful), the more upset I became, and the less I wanted to be with him.

I decided to be honest with him and tell him how I really felt about hearing about his ex-girlfriend. That I had begun to feel unwanted, and that I no longer wanted to be with him. He was surprised but also sad. He explained that he had thought I had been interested in hearing about her, because I had asked questions about her. From this point onwards he stopped talking about her and we were able to enjoy the remaining time we spent together.

I'd wanted to maintain a facade of being cool and unaffected rather than being honest. The result was that I began to distance myself from him, which at this point was the opposite of what I wanted. This meant that I tried to solve the "problem of feeling unwanted" wrongly by seeking to remove myself which defeated the very purpose, namely of wanting to be with him.

Only when I chose to be honest about my feelings did the opportunity arise to find the right solution which accorded with what I wanted.

The cliché that "the truth will set you free" is thus true, but in my opinion, it presupposes that you are able and willing to consciously accept "reality as it is" and limit your truth to "reality as it is" without coloring it through spurious interpretations.

In the case of the Dutchman, this meant accepting that I have a headache and nausea, and that I wanted him to help with shopping and cooking. That he is thoughtless, that he should know how bad I feel, or should offer to shop and cook, has nothing to do with reality. These are just my spurious interpretations about the situation.

It would be better to accept 'the reality of my sickness', express it to him and ask if he would mind doing the grocery shopping and cooking for us. Although this doesn't guarantee that he would oblige me, it would substantially increase the probability of receiving his help in the matter at hand. It would certainly be more relevant than addressing him up front by saying: "I think you are thoughtless and selfish because you haven't offered to do the groceries and cook. Can't you see that I'm sick?"

The thoughts and feelings that arise are present even if I try to avoid feeling them. They certainly don't vanish when I try to oppose them. On the contrary, 'what you resist does persist'.

The number of times in my life I have wanted to feel and think differently than I did is very high. And I have noticed that no matter how many times I have reminded myself that I shouldn't have certain emotions (for example, feeling insecure and vulnerable as above), it has never changed how I felt at that moment.

When I resist emotions that arise, I'm not always conscious of doing so because the reaction is so ingrained. A sure sign that I'm resisting my emotions is when my thoughts intensify and contain reproaches from others or myself, like when I started thinking negatively about the Dutchman as we left San Antonio. Such thoughts usually cover up difficult emotions that I'm unable to consciously feel in my body.

It's often overwhelming to consciously give space to what arises inside. However, it gets easier when I separate the emotions from the words or labels I attach to them and instead feel the physical sensations in the body directly. For example, when I separate the effect of agents such as anger, jealousy, envy, or guilt from the cause itself, and isolate and observe the physical effect in the body (such as a knot in the stomach, pressure on the chest, etc.), it's easier to give it space. Fully experiencing these emotions and their physical effect on the body and then acting on them is a very powerful way of resolving conflicts. It enables me to act in a manner that meets the challenge I face.

This doesn't mean I always get what I want. But once I accept "reality as it is" and am honest about it, it's no longer important whether things go my way or not. What is going on in my head is, after all, only thoughts – not reality.

Mexico City
MEXICO
Guatemala City
HONDURAS
Tegucigalpa
GUATEMALA
NICARAGUA
Managua
Cartagena
Panama City
San José
Mompox
COSTA RICA
VENEZUELA
Medellín
PANAMA
Bogotá
COLOMBIA
Quito
Guayaquil
ECUADOR
BRAZIL
Trujillo
PERU
Lima
Cusco
BOLIVIA
La Paz
Potosí
Tarija
Salta
500 km

CHAPTER 8

ACCIDENTS
Surrender

Nothing to win, nothing to lose.

LAO TZU

From La Quiaca in Argentina, I rode into Bolivia, where at the border I met two Belgian motorcyclists I'd first encountered in Patagonia and then in Salta. We spent five days together on the dusty gravel roads of the mountains of southern Bolivia. I'd now gained so much experience on gravel that I could easily follow two experienced motorcyclists. In Tupiza our paths parted, and I continued alone to Potosí.

Potosí was at an altitude of 13,000 feet, so it wasn't hot — especially not at night. At my hostel, I met two young English girls, and together we went to El Ojo del Inca — a hot spring shaped like a perfect circle with a diameter of 165 feet. An overseer at the hot spring said it was 820 feet deep, but I doubted that (which it later turned out not to be), but still, we were scared to plunge in. We couldn't see the bottom and the hot spring looked a bit suspicious. Only after the overseer had equipped us with a pair of bathing rings did we manage to get into the water.

Village in southern Bolivia.

A few weeks later, I rode into Peru, which became a mixed experience due to the unrest during the general strike. During the three weeks I spent in Peru traveling 2,175 miles, I didn't write a word in my diary. It wasn't because the landscape wasn't beautiful or that I didn't meet welcoming and friendly people along the way. The turmoil of the first days stayed on with me, which I managed to shake off only when I left Peru and rode into Ecuador.

The border with Ecuador was chaotic and a rather stressful affair. I had to take care of the custom papers to get my motorcycle into the country and at the same time keep a vigilant eye on the many men, so they didn't steal anything from the bike. As I stood in the customs office, through the window I could see a couple of men standing next to it, studying the map in the plastic pocket of the tank bag. I doubt it was the map they were interested in – but they

On the way to Tarija, Bolivia.

certainly were aware that I was watching them, which might have inhibited them from putting their hands into the bag.

Inside the customs office, I faced another problem. The customs officials claimed that I needed a specific document (which I didn't have) to get through customs. I'm sure I could have solved the problem by giving them a few dollars, but I chose the somewhat longer route of indulging in a dialogue. After some lengthy discussions, they handed me my customs papers and let me ride into Ecuador.

The first part of the road went through miles of plantain plantations (a green banana that tastes like a potato) and small villages. After riding through more than 1,000 miles of desert in Peru, it was a nice change to find myself among green and lush scenery. I rode through Guayaquil, Ecuador's largest city with 2.5 million inhabitants, and only once took a wrong turn, even though I didn't have a map of the city. I was pretty happy with that. My sense of direction had certainly gotten better on the trip.

I wanted to go to the beach, so I didn't consider making a stop in town. For the first time in several months, I was in warm weather and so I rode in just a T-shirt under my jacket. It was wonderful, even though the enjoyment that day was short-lived. It started to rain and by the time I reached the seaside resort of Montañita, I was soaked.

It wasn't difficult to find a place to stay and I stayed at the best hotel with a swimming pool. My room was huge with a balcony and a view of the Pacific Ocean. I lay in bed and read the Tao Te Ching while listening to the sound of the waves and birds. I needed to pamper myself. It was a palpable feeling that I had ridden quite a few miles lately.

The next day I continued to the nearby fishing village, Puerto López, where I went on a whaleboat excursion. We saw both whales and dolphins jumping, and it surprised me how great an experience it was. When I saw a killer whale jump out of the water, I felt dwarfed; I was deeply impressed with this immense and wonderful beast. Shortly after, a crowd of dolphins came close to the boat. I loved both the whales and the dolphins; I thought they looked cute and clever, although I could probably beat them at chess.

We went ashore on the island of Isla de la Plata, also known as the Cheap Galápagos, because it has rich wildlife and is a cheaper destination than the Galápagos. We walked around for three hours, and I was certainly not disappointed, perhaps because I wasn't burdened by any great knowledge of wildlife on our planet. We saw some strange birds with blue feet, which in form resembled a duck. The feet were large and lumpy, making it difficult for the birds to walk, but as soon as they took off, they transformed into elegant, streamlined creatures.

We also saw the birds with the blue feet in battle. One male had come a little too close to a pair, so the husband attacked the unwelcome intruder. I thought about how these birds had no choice but to live out their instincts. This is how it also seemed to be for us humans to the extent that we are identified with our thoughts and feelings. This was certainly true for me.

We also saw a bird where the males had a red bag under their beak which they inflated to attract females. Somewhat silly, but apparently it worked.

As it happened, the birds with the red bag were not the only ones using silly methods to attract attention from members of the opposite sex. Later that evening I got a reminder that a quick fix doesn't exist and that avoiding falling back into old habits requires persistent attention.

After the boat trip, I went out for dinner with a Spanish-Ecuadorian couple, a Frenchman and an American, whom I had met on the trip to Isla de la Plata. During dinner, I suddenly needed to point out that I was travelling alone by motorcycle. This sounds quite innocent – it was true after all – but the discomfort I felt upon mentioning it warned me of an attempt to show off. That it was an attempt to compensate for feeling insecure and not good enough. On the boat, the Frenchman had shown interest in me, and at dinner I wanted more of his attention. The result was quite the opposite.

On the way home

When I crossed the Equator, sixteen months had passed since I'd last set foot on the northern hemisphere. It was a nice feeling to be back. I spent a few more relaxing weeks in Ecuador and started searching the web for a plane ticket home from Los Angeles. I wasn't yet ready to buy it, but I knew I was getting closer to making a decision.

From Ecuador, I continued into Colombia. I'd been nervous about going there. Most reports about Colombia in the Danish media were about

The ride through Bolivia – La Paz.

crime and drugs, but during the trip I had met many travellers who had been there and who warmly recommended it.

During the six weeks I travelled around Colombia, I was greeted by an overwhelming openness and hospitality. Whenever I got lost in a city, I was often escorted onto the right path by Colombian motorcyclists, and I received several invitations to stay with people.

The first day in the country, however, I had to get used to the many police and military posts along the road. In the southern part, there was a lot of drug trafficking and every three miles I encountered a military post. However, whenever I was waved to the side, I was always greeted with curiosity and kindness, and no one tried to get money from me. At each bridge crossing a river, there was a small sandbag bunker on each side. In order to

North of La Paz, waiting to cross a small lake.

prevent anyone from trying to blow up a bridge, by law it was forbidden to stop on the bridges.

In the town of La Dorada, I met up with Camilo, a Colombian motorcyclist I'd met in northern Peru with his girlfriend Vicky. We rode together to Rionegro, where his family and girlfriend lived. It was nice to ride with Camilo. He was a good rider and I enjoyed following him and not having to think about route planning or anything else. After ten months alone on a motorcycle, I had begun to feel mentally fatigued. When we got to Rionegro, I saw Vicky jumping on the back of Camilo's motorcycle and could feel a tinge of envy. It would be nice if I could occasionally leave the handlebars to someone else's control.

On the way from La Dorada to Rionegro, Camilo and I visited the remains of Pablo Escobar's hacienda, Nápoles. Pablo Escobar was the leader of the Medellin cartel and the most brutal and infamous drug lord up through the eighties, not just in Colombia, but in the world. Camilo's father later told me how the businessmen, like himself, had been given a choice between *plata o plomo* – money or lead. That strategy helped make Pablo Escobar one of the wealthiest people in the world. From his hacienda until his death in 1993 – when he was shot by the police – he controlled his empire of drug trafficking and smuggling, extortion, murder, kidnapping, and bribery to such an extent that it destabilized Colombian society.

Above the entrance to the hacienda there was a small propeller plane, which according to Camilo was the first plane Escobar had used for cocaine smuggling to the United States. The hacienda stretched over 8 square miles of land, where Escobar had built several houses and artificial lakes, stored an extensive collection of vintage cars (of which I saw the burnt-out remains) and established a zoo – sixteen hippos and a few zebras still lived on the hacienda. Two hippos had fled and now lived in Río Magdalena, a major river nearby. Surely, I wasn't tempted to go for a swim there.

I had no doubt that the hacienda had once been one of the most luxurious spots on earth. According to Camilo, the land now belonged to the Colombian state, which had plans to build a prison and re-establish the zoo. A rather special combo.

From Hacienda Nápoles we rode on to the Río Claro, which was a crystal-clear river, as the name suggests. We parked the motorcycles and got out our swimwear for a cooling dip. It was 104°F.

Camilo suggested jumping into the river from a ledge. I estimated the fall to be about 16 feet and was therefore primarily concerned about whether the river was deep enough. Camilo assured me that it was, so I went to the edge and jumped in without hesitation. As I hovered in the air, I discovered to my great horror that it wasn't 16 feet but closer to 28 feet. At touchdown, I was so tense with fear in my neck and jaw that the landing was pretty painful

Pablo Escobar's hacienda with Camilo, Colombia.

– I had sore teeth and a sore jaw for the rest of the day and realised that my days of foolhardy stunts were over.

After a week with Camilo's family, I said goodbye and continued to Mangangué, where a ferry crossed the Río Magdalena to the historic town of Santa Cruz de Mompox. I arrived when it was dark and found a cheap hotel with the help of a Colombian motorcyclist. Perhaps a little too cheap.

In my room there were ants everywhere – even on the bed – so I asked for another one. Since the rest of the available rooms were all air-conditioned (unlike mine), the receptionist wanted a higher price for a switch. Here I informed him that this wasn't my problem, and he quickly realised that he wouldn't have much luck discussing with the tired, Danish woman. My new room with air-conditioning and at the same price as the first one was ant-free.

In addition to the bed, there was an elongated mirror that hung so low that the image didn't reveal my head. It wasn't the first time I had encountered this problem in South America.

I woke up the following morning at 5:30 a.m. at the sound of my alarm clock to catch the boat at 7 a.m. The night before, I had inquired around town about the ferry's departure time and received four different answers: 6 a.m., 6.30 a.m., 7 a.m. and 7.30 a.m. Two had answered 7 o'clock with some conviction in their voices.

I arrived at the ferry berth at 6.40 a.m. and was told that the ferry had already taken off, even though it wasn't scheduled to depart until 7 a.m. The other of the two ferries had broken down, and therefore the only operating ferry departed as soon as it was full.

I was instead offered to cross the river in a smaller boat, but when I saw it, I had a hard time imagining how it could be done. It looked like an overgrown canoe. However, the men around me, who oversaw loading the boat, assured me that it could easily handle the weight of my motorcycle.

It was rather distressing crossing the river. When my motorcycle was on board, I found a place further back, where I could observe how the loading of both motorcycles (smaller than mine but still), packages and people continued. Even some locals began to express concern about the heavy load – which is never a good sign.

With sixty people, ten motorcycles and a lot of luggage, the boat was pushed ashore. A gasp for air went through the passengers. A woman loudly expressed her nervousness and I quietly chimed in. The two men next to me assured me that there was nothing to be afraid of, even though their body language told me otherwise. I decided to try to enjoy the ride as much as possible. We were already at full speed with the help of the strong current, and it was no use causing a stir.

On the way to Mompox, Colombia.

My fragile calmness, however, lasted only until we had to cross the strong current to reach a smaller branch of the river – and along the way pass a sizable, floating scrub. With approximately 8 inches of freeboard, it wouldn't take much before the boat tilted and took in water, but miraculously we got through. After 30 minutes, my fellow passengers and I were finally able to breathe a sigh of relief. Everyone quickly jumped ashore, and a couple of men helped me unload my motorcycle.

I stayed one day in Mompox, a charming town from the Spanish colonial era. Although I usually explored the villages I visited on foot, I made an exception here. It was simply too hot and humid, so I hired a small scooter taxi to show me around which allowed me to sit in the shade with a pleasant breeze against my face.

From Mompox I proceeded to Cartagena. That required a crossing of the Río Magdalena again, but this time I was determined to wait for the big ferry, no matter how long it may take. Although it was much larger, it didn't appear to be much more secure. It looked like a giant, rusty raft and, like the overgrown canoe, was over-filled – now also including trucks.

The wait for the ferry meant it had become late afternoon, when I reached the other side of the river. The early evening horizon was dark gray and occasionally lit by long, slender lightning bolts. I wouldn't reach Cartagena until dark.

At six o'clock I was stopped at a major Retén Militar, as the police and military posts were called, at the town of El Carmen de Bolivar two hours south of Cartagena. "Wow!" said one of the five camouflage-clad men around me upon discovering it was a woman on the motorcycle.

A man in civilian clothes came over and asked to see my papers. He turned out to be the head of the Colombian intelligence department in El Carmen de Bolivar. He had the best eyes I had seen in a long time, and I had no doubt that I was looking at an honest human being. He reminded me of Mariano.

I asked him if it was dangerous to ride when it was dark, and he assured me it was safe. However, this hadn't always been the case, he told me. For the previous two years, the country road between El Carmen de Bolivar and Cartagena had been closed between 6 p.m. and 6 a.m. due to guerrillas nightly looting cars and trucks. The road had been reopened only nine months earlier after years of fighting between Colombian police, military, and the guerrillas.

The region south of Cartagena, concentrated around El Carmen de Bolivar, was at this time one of three high-risk areas in Colombia, where many fights had taken place. El Carmen de Bolivar was one of the most impoverished provincial towns in Colombia, where organized crime and solid cooperation with the guerrillas for many years had shaped the daily lives of the town's 35,000 inhabitants.

During the past six years, 190 police officers and soldiers were killed here in battles against guerrilla forces. The guerrillas were thought to have been reduced from 2,000 people to about 500. They lived in hiding just a 50-minute drive from the town in the surrounding mountains.

However, I felt safe after the man in the civilian outfit assured me that I was safe. When he'd finished looking through my papers, I put the motorcycle in gear and waved goodbye. Shortly after, the darkness and rain prevailed, but the real danger that confronted me came from somewhere else: the big trucks heading south, which didn't dim the high beam for oncoming vehicles. I couldn't see a thing, when I was blinded by their lights and I all I could do was hope that I didn't hit one of the many holes in the road.

I arrived quite tired in Cartagena after overcoming the last obstacle which was losing my way in the dark on the outskirts of the city. It wasn't because I'd ridden a long distance; it was only 150 miles, but the ride in the dark had drained my last bit of strength. I found a hostel with a garage in the historic part of town and went for a walk in the warm evening air.

I immediately fell in love with the old, colorful neighborhood. Many of the townhouses were newly renovated and stood side by side in strong yellow, red, and blue colors. Most of the roofs were clad with rustic-looking red tiles. The woodwork was painted white, and on the balconies, green plants with pink flowers abounded over the railings.

The streets were narrow, and the traffic was limited so I could stroll around without traffic noise and car fumes. The many squares with palm trees were either centered around illuminated fountains that offered an oasis in the evening heat or filled with chairs, tables, and umbrellas from the many cafés and restaurants. The old town was surrounded by a thick wall overlooking the Caribbean Sea and Cartagena's modern part with its skyline. At the end

Cartagena, The Walled City, Colombia.

of one of the long walls was erected a small pavilion where locals in close embrace danced the Dominican dance bachata to loud music.

I spent a few weeks on the Caribbean Sea in and around Cartagena and then headed for Bogotá. The Darién Gap, the northwestern part of Colombia adjacent to Panama, is difficult to navigate and populated only by a few indigenous groups and guerrillas. There are not many roads; the Pan-American Highway, which runs through all of North and South America, also pauses here. The area is covered with dense rainforest, mountains and rivers and is certainly not meant for a motorcycle or any other vehicle for that matter.

In Bogotá, I booked a space for my motorcycle on a cargo plane to Panama City, and only when the motorcycle was ready to be loaded, did I buy my own plane ticket. After a year and a half in South America, I'd learned to take my precautions. Things take time – especially when authorities are involved.

The shipping cost was 1,000 dollars, including the preparation of shipping documents, which the shipping company took care of. The money had to be paid in cash. I was relieved not to have to fill in the many forms myself. When I showed up at the freight company at the airport, however, I was told that I would have to get the papers stamped with the customs authorities myself. How long could it take? Six hours, including a customs and drug inspection of the motorcycle.

I sank into the seat on the commercial flight and found myself at ease. From my window seat I had a breathtaking view of the northern tip of the South American continent and the dark red sunset on the horizon. It was an unfamiliar but welcoming feeling to be transported somewhere without having to do anything myself. A year and a half had passed since I'd last sat on a plane.

I felt sad in having to say goodbye to this place in the world that had brought me so many experiences and encounters. What stood out most clearly in my memory was the help offered and kindness with which I'd been met by people I didn't know and for the most part would never see again. The reality I had encountered in South America was in stark contrast to the stories about the continent that seemed to occupy most journalists in Denmark and the rest of Europe.

The accident

On my first day on the motorcycle in Panama, I got a taste of what the riding experience would be like in Central America: rain every single day. Most of the time it wasn't even warm. Riding with leaky rainwear didn't help – I was soaked from the hip down after every encounter with the rain.

The many border crossings in Central America were also quite stressful. Because they were usually busy and full of people, it was tiresome to keep an eye on the motorcycle while arranging the customs papers.

Many were young men who offered travellers help filling out the forms, but I wasn't convinced that they were actually able to help, so each time I ended up doing it myself.

Moreover, two additional steps in the border crossing procedure were added in certain countries in Central America that I hadn't encountered in South America. First, I had to hand in a photocopy of a newly stamped document, which I'd received from the customs officials. This meant that I had to find a photocopier, which was located at some distance from the office where I had to hand in the copy. Second, the motorcycle tires had to be sprayed with a toxic substance to prevent any animal diseases from being carried across the border. Obviously, I had to pay for this treatment, but not at the same counter where I got the customs papers arranged.

Something else that stressed me out in Central America was the sight of guards with shotguns at several petrol stations – especially in Honduras. At each of the petrol stations where I stopped, I was met by a heavily armed guard. I did sense that they were standing there with good reason.

I had begun to wish that the whole journey would come to an end. While in Bogotá, I'd bought my return flight ticket from Los Angeles on December 10, with five days in New York. This meant that I would arrive in Copenhagen precisely one year after I'd embarked on my motorcycle trip from Buenos Aires. I daydreamed about being at home in Denmark in my own bed and not having to find a new place to sleep every night.

Mexico City.

I mobilized the last energy left in my tired body and survived the many hours in the pouring rain on the motorcycle. When I got to Mexico City, I only had an easy week's riding left. The rain had even stopped. My goal was within reach, and I vividly imagined what it would feel like to ride into Los Angeles after a year on a motorcycle through South and Central America.

I spent five days in Mexico City. In Panama, I'd met another traveller at my hostel who had put me in touch with a Danish guy, Jens, who lived in Mexico City. As I approached the capital, I contacted him, and he immediately invited me to stay with him. It was over four months ago that I had last spoken Danish – in La Paz in Bolivia, where I'd met a Danish couple at my hostel.

I cannot describe the joy I experienced in speaking my mother tongue again. I kept saying to Jens: "I speak Danish, I speak Danish! Can you hear me speak Danish?" He could, but he wasn't impressed. To me, it was like receiving a big gift. Suddenly I could express everything I wanted to say. I could invent new words; I could joke and make puns effortlessly. I could swear, be silly, and I could talk effortlessly.

I enjoyed the Danish company, and we spent a couple of joyous days together. However, I didn't get much sleep. I hadn't slept well for many weeks and mentally I felt like I'd been sucked into a black hole. I desperately needed sleep to gather enough energy for the last part of the journey, but I didn't consider staying longer in Mexico City to rest. I had a plan, and I was going to stick to it. With limited energy available, my autopilot and steely focus from the old days had taken control. I was going to reach my goal – no matter what.

When I woke up in the morning I'd planned to ride north. I'd only got a few hours of sleep, and when I opened my eyes, my first thought was, "I'm not able to ride today. It's impossible." Then I started crying.

Slowly I started packing and making plans for the day. I decided to get out of Mexico City and find a quiet hotel in the countryside where I could get a good night's sleep. This way, the worst traffic in and around the city would be behind me and I would be ready for a long day on the motorcycle the following morning.

I had no map of Mexico City, so I wasn't sure whether I was on the right path when I encountered the first motorway entrance. I stopped and waved at a passing motorcyclist urging him to halt. Luck was on my side since he was heading in the same direction as me and offered to guide me out of town. I just had to follow his lead.

We rode onto the highway and at that moment I felt relieved. My worries about finding my way out of the city without a map now seemed silly. I had an excellent human guide to bring me safely and smoothly out of the largest city on the North American continent with 21 million inhabitants. It couldn't get much easier.

Just as these thoughts crossed through my head, a small red car in the middle lane suddenly took a quick turn to reach an exit on the right side, crossing the inner lane where I was. The left side of my handlebar got a jolt, and for what seemed like an eternity, I struggled to keep my balance. Unfortunately, I didn't make it.

During the crash I blacked out. The next thing I was aware of was the most intense pain I'd ever experienced. A moment later the pain was gone, and it felt as if I was outside of my body, hanging somewhere to the left above it. At that moment, the pain was so intense that I couldn't feel it. Everything became one as if I ceased to exist.

A moment later, I felt the pain with undiminished strength – I was without a doubt back in my own body. I must have screamed like crazy, for the people who had gathered around me didn't dare approach me. From a safe distance, someone shouted at me not to move. The first thing I did when I heard this was precisely to move; the pain came from my left leg, and I had to feel if it was still there. After being hit, I'd slid along the road until my left knee hit a curb at the exit and stopped my slide. The knee had been pinched between the curb and the motorcycle.

I was in a state of shock. I couldn't believe this had happened. One week before I was at the finish line, but now I'd been hit by a car.

Slowly, my crying subsided and those around me came closer. The motorcyclist, who had offered to guide me out of the city, had called for an ambulance. The driver of the small red car that had hit me came up to me and took full responsibility for the accident – an unusual occurrence in Latin America, where many drive without insurance and therefore take flight after traffic accidents.

The ambulance arrived and the paramedics asked me which hospital I wanted to be taken to. I had no idea, so I asked if they could recommend one, but they couldn't; it was against the rules to recommend a hospital to an injured person. To my great luck, a Mexican on a Harley motorcycle came to my rescue. Luís, as he was called, had passed the scene of the accident, and had stopped to offer his help. He let me borrow his cellphone so I could contact the Danish embassy in Mexico. By chance, I had the embassy's telephone number in my tank bag (these were the days before smartphones). The parliamentary election was taking place in Denmark, and a few days earlier I'd been to the embassy to do my civic duty and vote. A diplomat at the embassy recommended that I go to Hospital Español.

Still in shock, I was laid on a stretcher and ushered into the ambulance. Luís made sure I got all my belongings from the motorcycle with me. He promised he would take care of my motorcycle and today I can thank him for still having it. He waited several hours for a truck to pick it up and followed it to a workshop (which was situated 100 feet from where Jens lived). Here he was given the papers on the motorcycle's handover, which meant that it was beyond the reach of the long, corrupt arms of the police.

When I was in the ambulance, I thought my main worries were over, but it turned out that they were just about to begin. The driver of the little red car had called his insurance company, and the company had sent a man to the scene of the accident to speak – not to their customer, the policyholder, but to me. I was in shock again. I was alone, more than 6,000 miles away from my family and friends, lying in an ambulance in Mexico City on a motorway. How could anyone think I was in the mood to talk to a representative of an insurance company?

First, the insurance man tried to persuade me to go to another hospital, claiming that his company wouldn't cover the cost of my treatment at Hospital Español. It wasn't on their list of approved hospitals, he said. Crying, I told him I would only let the ambulance take me to Hospital Español. I knew nothing of the other hospitals, and I was determined to stick to the embassy's recommendation.

I had the best travel insurance that money could buy. I thought that if the Mexican insurance company wouldn't pay, then my company certainly would. And if they wouldn't, then I would. I didn't intend to risk my health because of a rude insurance man.

My reasoning didn't reach Mr. Insurance, and it was only when I began to cry loudly and seemed to be out of control that it dawned on him that the woman on the stretcher had no intention of giving in.

He left the ambulance but came back a moment later – he apparently didn't want to give up either. This time he handed me a piece of paper, which he asked me to sign. My first reaction was speechlessness. My crying increased in strength as I tried to explain that I wasn't able to sign anything. I turned my head, looked the other way, and let many tears and snot run out of my eyes and nose.

Finally, the insurance man disappeared, and as the ambulance set in motion, one of the paramedics took my hand and said, "It was very wise of you not to sign that piece of paper."

Now my tears ran free. I wept profusely, not because of pain – my leg kept a surprisingly low profile – but because the consequence of the accident dawned on me: that I wouldn't reach the goal I'd set for myself. A goal that felt right to me, and not because it looked good on my resumé.

I tried to explain this to the paramedics, but I doubt what I said made sense. One of them kept holding my hand. It was a small gesture, but at that moment, it meant everything – without it, I felt as if I would disappear from the face of the earth and be sucked into oblivion.

When we arrived at the hospital, I was subjected to several examinations, which lasted many hours. I'd been more than lucky and hadn't broken anything; the doctors who examined me were amazed. The encounter with the curb followed by a hard squeeze from the motorcycle had only left me with a large hematoma around my left knee and a yellow and blue body.

After the examinations, I was taken to a solitary room in the emergency section, where three younger doctors were present, while a fourth bandaged my left leg. A woman from the hospital administration came by and asked for the requisite insurance related information. Earlier in the day, the diplomat from the Danish embassy in Mexico City had visited me at the hospital. From his mobile phone, I had called my insurance company in Denmark, who promised me that they would cover all expenses. I didn't have to worry about anything.

I gave the admin woman my insurance information along with the phone number of their 24-hour telephone service and let out a sigh of relief. It was nine o'clock in the evening. Nine hours had passed since the accident.

Months of inadequate sleep and the extreme exhaustion both physically and mentally of being almost a year on a motorcycle now surfaced, adding an extra dimension to the pain and confusion surrounding the accident. I felt beyond weak.

I asked to go to the toilet. A nurse gave me a bed pan, but I insisted on having enough strength to walk myself. That turned out not to be the case, and instead I was helped into a wheelchair. The effort of lifting my body from the wheelchair to the commode almost made me faint. When I was taken back to my bed, I felt as if I'd run a marathon. A doctor came by and placed an intravenous drip in my right arm connected to a bag of yellow fluid.

The admin woman showed up again and told me she couldn't get hold of my insurance company. Therefore, I had to pay myself. I was surprised to hear that, but since my capacity to argue – which under normal circumstances is considerable – had been much diminished by the recent turn of events, I didn't care to argue with her. Instead, I gave the woman my credit card and expected the problem to go away.

Ten minutes later she came back and informed me that my credit card had been declined. I realised that the amount she had tried to withdraw on the card far exceeded the monthly amount I had available. I told her I would call my bank the following day and get the limit raised. Due to the time difference, I couldn't get hold of them right away. She replied that if I didn't pay immediately, I would have to leave the hospital.

Was there no end to bad news this day?

While I was trying to absorb the latest developments, shedding more tears, a female doctor, whom I hadn't seen before, came by to tell me that a nurse would soon remove the intravenous drip. It was now 11 o'clock in the evening, and the hospital staff was apparently of the opinion that I was ready to be discharged. I had a different view of my condition.

I couldn't walk and I had no friends or family in Mexico City to stay with. The day before the accident, Jens had left town on a week-long business trip to Monterrey in northern Mexico. A Chilean friend of Jens', Arturo, whom I had met three days before the accident at a concert, had come by the hospital in the afternoon. I had his phone number and had called him from Luís' cell phone at the accident scene. I had no idea if I could stay with him. If I left the hospital alone and ended up in the wrong taxi late at night in Mexico City I would be finished.

Half an hour later, the female doctor came by again and asked if the nurse had removed my drip. It was only then that it dawned on me that they actually intended to let me leave the hospital in the condition I was in.

Over my dead body was I going to get their help to leave! From now on I would take charge of the situation myself. I started crying loudly and shouted that if they didn't remove the drop immediately, I would rip it out of my arm myself. At the same time, I tried to get out of the hospital bed on the opposite side of where the drop was attached. I wanted to get as far away from this hospital as possible. If they thought it was okay to treat their patients this way, they were pitiably wrong, and I was furious.

The amount of noise and commotion I created caused several doctors and nurses to enter my room. A few minutes later, the admin woman came back with a document that she asked me to sign – if I did, the hospital would let me stay. Crying, I put an unreadable doodle on the paper, even though I didn't understand what I had just committed to. All I knew was that I didn't have the strength to find a new place to stay.

At one o'clock at night, I finally got something to eat and drink. At that moment, it felt like the best meal I'd ever had. I doubt if that was the case. When I finished eating, I pushed the tray with the empty plate away and fell asleep.

The following week, the admin woman dutifully came by my room every day asking for payment. She repeated the threat that I would have to leave the hospital if I didn't pay. This thought was so overwhelming that she might as well have pointed a gun at me and threatened my life. I couldn't handle even the slightest change.

I wrote emails and called my insurance company in Denmark every day. Every time they told me that they would take care of the payment and that one of their Spanish-speaking agents in Miami was on the case. They couldn't understand why the hospital kept asking me for money.

On the seventh day at the hospital, the admin woman came by while I was talking to the insurance agent in Miami. He asked to speak to her. I don't know what he said to her, but from my bed I could observe that her face became pale. The only words that came out of her mouth were the occasional *si, si...* until she hung up. That was the last time I saw her. I can't say that I missed her even though I wasn't overrun by visitors during my hospital stay.

The first three days in the hospital I spent crying. I pretended I was okay when the nurses came by. I didn't want to talk to them about what had happened. My insurance company had asked if I needed to speak to a crisis psychologist, but I didn't even consider it. Not because of pride. I was just convinced it wasn't necessary.

I wasn't yet willing to give up finishing my journey. I still intended to reach my goal and ride to Los Angeles even though I couldn't walk, every inch of my body was exhausted, and mentally I was wrapped in a thick fog.

On the third day, I finally gave up on continuing the journey. I accepted that under no circumstances was I able to ride a motorcycle. Whether I wanted to or not, my journey had ended in Mexico City one week before I was supposed to reach my goal. I surrendered. I had to fly home from Mexico City as soon as possible.

At that moment, I realised that nothing had changed since the accident. My immediate experience of who I am – without thoughts and stories of goals and worth – was the same in the hospital as it had been before the accident when I was sitting on my motorcycle.

The only change was the story I told about myself and my journey. For the first time in my life, I clearly saw that this narrative had nothing to do with who I am. It neither defined nor limited who I am. Whatever happened in the narrative, it would never be more than that: a good or bad story, depending on what mood I was in.

From then on, I felt relieved and grateful to be in the hospital. Now I had a legitimate reason to let others help me – I didn't have to lift a finger. If I needed help, I could ring a bell. The meals were served in bed and my bed was made for me. Every decision was out of my hands and that was exactly what I needed. I loved it.

Arturo visited and he was sweet to hold my hand and be there for me. Luís and his wife also came by to see me and brought the papers for my motorcycle. And when Jens was back in Mexico City, he brought a Carlsberg beer (not that I drank much of it) and pushed me around the hospital in a wheelchair at high speed while teasing me with my thick leg. It was just what I needed.

There is only now

Past and future manifest themselves in the present merely as thoughts about what has happened and what could happen. But life as such unfolds in the present. Therefore, I can only experience the true joy of being alive when my attention is anchored here and now.

Even though I'd only set daily goals during the journey, I'd often been uncomfortable trying to reach the next town. When I felt the first signs of hunger while riding, I didn't stop to eat. I kept riding for several hours until I'd reached my goal of the day. Only then did I feel that I had "time" to eat, and at that time my body was so exhausted that when I started eating, I couldn't stop even when satiated.

When I felt cold, I didn't stop immediately to put on more clothes. Instead, I kept riding on until the cold had made my limbs numb. If I had to go to the toilet, I kept riding on until my bladder was about to burst. Even when I was exhausted, I forced myself to keep going. I had to keep going until I reached my goal. Only when I was at the finish line did my thoughts tell me I could allow myself to relax.

Shortly before I reached the destination of the day, however, I invariably experienced a soothing silence that allowed me to enjoy the moment. Only then did the arresting thought that I could only relax when I had reached my goal, let go of me.

Often, my worries, for example, about crashing in deserted areas and not being found, had created so much noise in my head that I wasn't aware of this silence. Not because my concerns weren't real. To have a crash in a deserted area and lie injured for many hours could happen. I didn't have a personal GPS tracking device with me; I was alone, and no one knew where I was. Despite the danger being hypothetical, I still couldn't relax. It was only a tormenting mind game and the background reality was that I was hitherto unharmed. The more I was preoccupied with these thoughts, the greater the risk of a crash (my full attention wasn't where I was), and the further away I was from experiencing the silence and joy that were to be found in the present moment.

When I was close to the planned destination of the day and I became aware of this silence, I knew that it had been present from the beginning of the trip – not in every moment, but as every moment. I just hadn't noticed it. It often amazed me how I'd managed to overlook it. In the hospital in Mexico City, I suddenly understood why. It was because I'd believed that the feeling of silence and joy was a consequence of having reached my day's goal. Though a logical reasoning, it was nevertheless utterly misleading.

In the hospital, when I gave up on reaching my goal - to achieve something other than what was — I experienced a silence and joy equal to that I would feel, had I reached my goal. It was the absence of the desire to achieve anything other than what was in that moment that was the real cause of the satisfaction, silence, and joy I experienced.

San Francisco
USA
New York
Los Angeles
MEXICO
Mexico City
500 km

CHAPTER 9

THE FINISH LINE
Share your Joy

> Most of the beautiful moments in life are moments when you are expressing your joy, not when you are seeking it.
>
> SADHGURU

After ten days, I was discharged from the hospital with a pair of crutches. Due to the hemorrhage in my left leg and the increased risk of a blood clot that a flight might cause, I had to wait two more weeks to go home. I found a hotel close to Jens and took a taxi to the hospital every other day, where I received physiotherapy.

I was still weak, and as time went on, I had a hard time keeping up my spirits. The awareness of silence and joy quietly began to slip back into the background. Jens noticed that I wasn't feeling great and asked if I wanted to go to Acapulco, where he and a friend were attending a wedding. I could sit in the back of the car with my big leg and then relax in the house by the beach they were staying at while they attended the wedding party.

I felt overwhelmed by the thought of leaving my hotel room and I tried to decline politely. Jens, however, informed me that they would come by the next afternoon at five o'clock to pick me up and asked me to be ready.

I'm thankful he insisted on my going because that was exactly what I needed. While Jens and his friend were at the wedding, I hobbled around on the beach in the sunshine with my injured leg. Few people were out on the beach and some of them discreetly looked at my deformed leg. Jens continued with his well-meaning teasing — he thought my leg looked gross when I tried to bend it. So that was exactly what I tried to do every time he looked at it.

One month after the accident, I was back in Denmark.

The first two weeks I spent in my apartment, I resisted moving in. I postponed picking up from my brother's place the boxes containing my personal belongings. Finally, when I did pick them up, I delayed unpacking them. I sat in my empty apartment and felt somewhat alienated.

I simultaneously felt that nothing had changed since I'd left twenty-one months earlier, and yet everything had changed. I did not feel like seeing my family and friends. I cried without knowing why. Often, I would walk down the street and suddenly feel tears welling up. Then I would hurry back home.

When I was out shopping, I got nauseous from being surrounded by food and often left the supermarket without buying anything. Sometimes I felt dead inside. At other times I felt ecstatic. I had no idea how to navigate the familiar surroundings. Everything seemed so familiar, and yet I didn't know how to cope with being home again.

I went to the doctor to have my leg examined and briefly told her about the accident and my emotional disorientation. She told me that it was a natural reaction due to the physical and mental trauma I had suffered and that what I was experiencing was post-traumatic stress.

Slowly things began to change. I took one step at a time and refrained from worrying about the future. I was aware that I had limited energy available and that it was best to avoid overburdening myself with new chores and projects. I allowed myself to recover from the accident. Instinctively I knew that it was a process I couldn't hasten. On the journey, I had learned how to deal with complex thoughts and feelings which made it significantly easier to get through the discomfort without losing my footing.

After a month in Denmark, thoughts of returning to Mexico City to complete the journey began to emerge.

At this point, I still had no idea what I wanted to do with my life. While travelling, I had thought that when I returned to Denmark, I would have found my calling. I had often felt an inner pressure to come up with a set plan for life. But the stronger this pressure became, the more I had feared returning home.

During the last two months of the journey, the uncertainty and worries about the future had begun to hog my attention. As it happened, the accident had elbowed out these worries, making me focus on what was going on in the present. In every conceivable way, the accident, which at first glance was the worst that could happen, had been a source of contemplation and healthy introspection.

I had returned home with a knee the size of a basketball and a plan for the future of the same calibre as the one a goldfish would be able to conceive. I had more unanswered questions than when I left. My big plan for the future was farther away than it had ever been. At first glance, it seemed that my journey in this respect had been a failure, but actually, the missing plan had set me free – exactly as I wished for.

Now I was in a situation where I had freed myself from the shackles of my own plan and pressure. That meant that I could live the life I wanted to live without thinking about whether I fitted in or reached a particular goal in the future. When I worked as a lawyer, it felt selfish to allow myself to do what felt right. What I now understood clearly was the absurdity in expecting others to live the way I thought was right – and vice versa.

My desire to return to Mexico City to complete the journey did not have to be measured against a big plan – neither by me nor others. However, I had several concerns.

First, I no longer wanted to run away from my problems. If another motorcycle trip was an attempt to escape from myself, then I did not want to go. I felt I had become strong enough to handle whatever might come. Secondly, I was afraid to ride a motorcycle. I had narrowly escaped from the encounter with the red car without any permanent injuries, but I could very nearly have been killed. Was I willing to risk my life to complete a journey that was just a plan created in my head? Maybe the accident was a signal that I should stop riding a motorcycle before it was too late. And third, it would soon be necessary to earn money again.

Since the accident, I'd been in contact with a motorcyclist, Chris Dawe, in Pennsylvania, USA, who had been a wonderful support to me. On the website of Horizons Unlimited, a forum for motorcycle travellers, I had asked some practical questions regarding my motorcycle, and Chris was amongst those who had answered.

In an email to Chris, I mentioned that I wanted to return to Mexico City to complete the trip but that I urgently needed to earn some money. He suggested I give talks about my journey through Latin America to other motorcyclists – he knew of other motorcycle riders who gave such talks with great success.

So far, it hadn't occurred to me that anyone would be interested in hearing about my motorcycle trip. Nevertheless, the idea of sharing my experiences with others touched a chord within me. I had managed to take the plunge and travel alone through Latin America on a motorcycle. If I, of all people – without knowing much about riding a motorcycle, without speaking Spanish and with almost no experience of travelling alone – could manage such a journey, anyone who wanted to, could do so. It seemed like a good message to share with others.

I thus began to see my journey in a new light. Without stopping to think if I was on the right track, I started committing to words the lessons I had learned. I tried to find an angle and a platform for sharing my experiences with others. Before long, I was writing the text for a website. I hired a web designer, asked friends for advice, and after three months in Denmark, the website was ready. At the time, I didn't know how to put my talk together and what it should contain. However, I was not that concerned, as I knew what the core message would be, and I felt it was sufficient to get started.

At the same time, I seriously began to consider returning to Mexico City. Temporally I was just one week from reaching Los Angeles and I still wanted to go there. But it seemed silly to ride the short distance from Mexico City to Los Angeles and then fly home again. Instead, I got the idea of riding across the United States to New York.

My worries about whether I was trying to escape my problems disappeared – as opposed to the fear of riding a motorcycle. I had no idea how I was going to overcome it and whether I should.

I chose a pragmatic way to clear up this doubt. I had to find out what became of my motorcycle in Mexico City. After I was discharged from the hospital in Mexico City, I went to the workshop to see Señor Dakar. I had talked to the guy in charge at the workshop, Luís, whom I immediately felt I could trust, and he had promised me that my motorcycle would be repaired and ready when I needed it.

But three months later, I had not received any news. I did not even know whether it was still in the workshop. From experience, I knew that anything could happen in Latin America. Maybe it had disappeared. If my motorcycle had not been repaired, or if it had disappeared, the dilemma to go or not to go to Mexico City resolved itself. No motorcycle – no motorcycle trip.

I wrote an email to Luís at the workshop and asked about the motorcycle. I promised myself that if I received an answer, I would listen to my first spontaneous reaction to it, no matter what it was. If at a later point in time I doubted my decision, I would stick to my first spontaneous reaction.

The following day I received an answer. My motorcycle was ready and waiting for me and Luís wrote that he was looking forward to seeing me again. I felt so happy that I jumped around in my apartment to vent the joy in me. I immediately bought a plane ticket to Mexico City with a return ticket from New York. A month later, I was on my way to finishing the final stage of my journey.

Back in the saddle

Four months after the accident, I was in the saddle again. BMW Motorrad in Denmark had sponsored me with new riding gear and a helmet after the accident, so I was well protected for the upcoming trip. I started the motorcycle and listened to the engine. Then I took a deep breath, put it in gear, slowly releasing the clutch and turning the throttle gently. My body balanced the motorcycle into a smooth, familiar rhythm.

A moment later, I was gripped by a strong undercurrent of fear. Every muscle in my body was tense. Every turn was a battle to ward off yet another imagined crash. It was as if I was in a horror movie where I wasn't on the surviving team.

During the first month of riding, I wasn't able to enjoy the journey. I was terrified of being hit by a car again. I tried to minimize the time I spent in the saddle, which can be perceived to be counterproductive on a motorcycle trip. A few times I experienced the joy of riding, but it quickly was drowned

Baja California, Mexico.

in the growing fear of sudden death involving a large truck, my motorcycle, and myself.

Even when I arrived in Los Angeles after three weeks, I had a hard time enjoying reaching the goal I had set on the first part of the trip. When I arrived in San Francisco a week later, I was so paralyzed by fear that I couldn't continue. I stayed in town for a month with my Scottish friend, Paul, under the pretext of wanting to explore the city and its neighborhoods. That was partly true, but a deeper motivation to stay was the fear of another accident. I wasn't able to get rid of it and the accompanying thought that next time I wouldn't escape with an odd-sized leg and a bruised body.

In an attempt to overcome the fear, I decided to attend an off-road riding clinic in Hollister, south of San Francisco. I thought it might mitigate the fear even if my accident had not happened on gravel.

Halfway through the day, we were practicing wheelies (lifting the front wheel of the motorcycle). Kari, one of the owners of the BMW motorcycle dealership at Mountain View in Silicon Valley, demonstrated the exercise. I intently followed every one of his movements to be able to imitate him.

When it was my turn, I turned the throttle and tried to get the front wheel up. It didn't lift an inch. I twisted the throttle harder with the result that I instantly lost control of the motorcycle and rode straight into the gravel on the side of the track. The front wheel drilled its way into the gravel followed by my left knee that had taken a hit in the accident in Mexico City.

Several riders came over to me to make sure I was okay. With every single cell in my body, I struggled not to panic, and I managed to hold back most of the tears and force a brave smile on my face while the pain in my left knee was throbbing wildly. If I gave in to the pain and the mental images I saw in my head of a smashed knee, I would not be able to maintain my composure.

I stumbled off the track and tried not to think about what had just happened. I had hit my left knee – again. It had to be a sign that I should stop riding a motorcycle. A paramedic arrived and gave me ice for my knee. The frontal collision with the gravel meant that the knee had not been twisted, only bruised. I put ice on my knee and quickly felt the pain go away.

Instead of diminishing my fear of an accident, my outing to Hollister had intensified it, resulting in a bruised knee, and a significant mechanic's bill. The motorcycle's radiator looked as if it had been kicked in by Hulk.

However, I could not complain about the location, where the accident took place. I was surrounded by people who were more than willing to help me. I agreed with Kari to have my motorcycle repaired at his workshop in Mountain View. I also told him that I was starting up as a speaker and asked if he was interested in engaging me at a customer event. He wanted to talk to his partners and find out if it were possible to arrange something at short notice, and a few days later he called. I was scheduled for the following Friday. It gave me a week to prepare the content for my talk.

I started a brainstorming session with myself. My stunt at the dirt clinic illustrated that I wasn't an expert on riding techniques. I wouldn't attract many listeners if I claimed to be an expert in this field unless someone was interested in learning how to make their motorcycle look like it had been kicked in by Hulk. I didn't think this would be appreciated. It made me think of a quote from Hemingway, who wrote: "Whatever success I have had has been through writing what I know about." It seemed likely that this principle also applied to what one talks about.

What did I know about traveling on a motorcycle? It was a fact that I wasn't the best at riding a motorcycle, not the best at planning a motorcycle trip, not the first woman to ride a motorcycle alone through Latin America. What in the world should I talk about then? Suddenly it became clear to me: about all my mistakes.

My confidence instantly rose. What now? Naturally, I could not talk about all the mistakes I had made along the way, so I had to pick the best ones – whatever that meant. I decided to focus on the mistakes that had hurt me the most. I reviewed my journey and selected ten situations, where I had been most miserable.

Two days before my premiere, I had managed to put together a talk entitled 'Adventure riding through Latin America – The top 10 list of what not to do'. I had no idea if I would actually succeed in giving a coherent talk. For the first time in my life, I presented myself as I was. The talk was built on my own experiences and did not refer to wise books, legal rules, or expert panels.

When I arrived at the motorcycle dealership in Mountain View, I was surprisingly calm. The fact that I did not get paid for my talk certainly had an impact. How much could you expect from an amateur who shares her experiences for free? At worst, my audience would have to survive an hour's agony.

About eighty people turned up, and as I rounded off my talk, I was greeted by overwhelming applause. They seemed to like it – and all I had done was to honestly tell my own story. Afterwards, several of the participants came up to me and thanked me for sharing my experiences.

I had unsuccessfully gone to Hollister to overcome my fear of riding a motorcycle. Instead, I got the opportunity to give my first talk and experience that my knowledge was worth sharing. My plan of how things ought to progress had once again been disrupted by reality, and I could see that I was now able to easily let go of my plan and see what opportunities arose when it didn't pan out as intended.

However, my fear of riding a motorcycle was unchanged. Back in San Francisco, I still had the feeling that my crash on the dirt track was a clear message to stop tempting fate, to go home, to grow up, and forget about riding a motorcycle. It would be a self-imposed torture to continue the journey with the amount of fear I experienced. My inability to relax on the bike significantly increased the risk of another accident.

I called my good friend Ernest back in Denmark and told him about my paralyzing fear. I knew I could always count on his honest opinion. My account touched on all aspects of the anxiety I experienced, although "fruit and nut case" could have summed up my condition nicely. He listened intently as I explained, and when I finally stopped talking, he said: "Annette, as I see it, you have two choices: you can stop riding a motorcycle, or you can stop whining."

This was tough love; after all, I had been through a serious accident. But as I let his words sink in, I had no doubt he was right. And what was more

Highway 1, south of San Francisco, USA.

surprising was that I also knew that I was in no way willing to stop riding a motorcycle. It had all been a show. I had created a drama in my head and had gained quite a bit of attention on this account. Still, if I had to choose between my drama and riding a motorcycle, I had no doubt who would be the winner: Señor Dakar.

A few days later, I packed my motorcycle and crossed the Bay Bridge on my way east. The fear of another accident was behind me, and it hasn't surfaced since.

Reaching the finish line

During my journey across the States, I was at a major motorcycle event hosted by BMW Owners of America in the state of Wyoming in the northwestern part of the US. Here I gave another talk and met with my new motorcycle friends from Colorado, Chris and Erin, to whom Chris in Pennsylvania had introduced me. They asked, if I wanted to join them on a ride to Mato Tipila, also known as Devil's Tower, a sacred site for the Lakota Indians and the first national monument in the United States.

We were joined by three other motorcyclists, including a man who wore the same BMW motorcycle jacket as me. "Nice jacket," I said as he walked towards us. It turned out to be the top executive of BMW Motorrad in the United States.

At lunch, we chatted, and I told him that I had just started out as a speaker and asked him if he would like to hear my talk at BMW Motorrad's headquarters in New Jersey, just outside Manhattan. Yes, he would like to. I gave him my card and he promised to get back to me.

When I approached Manhattan two months later, I hadn't heard from him. I decided to pay a visit to BMW Motorrad HQ and enquire about him at the front desk. I was told that he was in a meeting, so I put down my card once more and wrote on the back that if he wanted to hear my talk, he could contact me. I would be in Manhattan for the next five days before returning to Denmark.

An hour later, on a hot summer day in late July, I arrived in New York City. Before I disappeared into the Lincoln Tunnel, I caught a glimpse of the Manhattan skyline; the skyscrapers looked small, almost unreal. Five minutes later, I reappeared on the other side of the Hudson River in the shadow of the tall buildings around me.

As I slowly moved through Manhattan's traffic, I tried to grasp that I had finally reached my goal. I didn't succeed. A deep relaxation spread through my body, and I felt like I was about to merge with everything that surrounded me.

Heading east, Death Valley, USA.

Argentina. Instead, I chose to tell half my life story before the traffic started moving again. I simply couldn't hold back the joy. I had to share it.

I rode to my motorcycle friends, Francine and David, in NoHo, to whom Chris in Pennsylvania had also introduced me. While I was unloading my luggage in the living room, my phone rang. It was a manager from BMW Motorrad USA who wanted to arrange a time for my talk at HQ. I was more than surprised – I could hardly believe that I had this opportunity to speak at BMW's HQ in the United States. We agreed that I would give a talk a day before my return trip. What better way to end my journey!

New York City at Central Park South, USA.

Home

The next day I returned home to Denmark. I had achieved what I had set out to do, and yes, it was extremely satisfying. I celebrated it with my family, and in the weeks after my return, I delighted in the joy of having reached my goal. However, I also knew that it neither changed anything fundamentally nor protected me against fear, anger, restlessness and all the other emotions I had spent many years trying to evade.

Therefore, it did not frighten me nor surprise me when the first restlessness of being at home surfaced. What now?

I turned my attention to my body trying to trace how the restlessness manifested itself. There was a tingling sensation in the stomach and a tremor throughout the body. After a while, it had almost disappeared. Without thinking about it, I took out my notepad and looked at it: I had to call my dentist to make an appointment for a dental checkup, put lights on my bicycle, buy a birthday present, and so on. Nothing could be more mundane. I looked at the list again and reflected: right now, this is the content of my life. What shall I do about it – resist it and try to get away or give it my full attention?

I gave it my full attention and immersed myself in everyday life. After all, calling my dentist didn't presuppose that I had a bigger plan for my life. I kept my focus on what I was doing without thinking about where I was going. This approach had worked the last time I returned home, and I sensed that something would probably show up if I took care of the things that were imminent with an immediacy of purpose.

And sure enough, before long, I got the idea to return to the States the following spring. I had left my motorcycle with Chris in Pennsylvania, 125 miles from New York. I felt that I wasn't done with long-distance motorcycle riding, and the journey across the States had shown me that it could easily be punctuated by delivering talks. I had gained sufficient experience now that I was confident enough to ask to get paid. While planning my next trip, I even got help unexpectedly: BMW Motorrad in the USA had decided to sponsor my talks at their motorcycle dealerships.

I had trusted that the answers would come when I let go of the desire to find certainty when in doubt. Not the answers to all my questions, but the answers to those that needed to be answered now.

Looking back, I understand why my fear of the future grew, the closer I got to the end of my motorcycle trip in Latin America. I had looked in all the wrong places for answers. Ironically, it was not until three days before my accident in Mexico City that I got the first clear hint as to where I should turn my attention.

I had attended a concert in Mexico City given by Michala Petri and Lars Hannibal, which my friend Jens had organized. Michala Petri is a world-renowned Danish musician playing the recorder. I knew of Michala Petri but had never heard her play live. I enjoyed the concert immensely and was very moved by their performance. It was done with the utmost sensitivity, storytelling, and lightness.

But at the same time, I also felt sad. I knew that Michaela Petri had started playing the recorder as a three-year-old and that by this time she was in her late forties. She had spent more than forty years getting this good, and it was no secret that she had worked hard and practised many hours every day. I was wondering if I would ever be good at anything after leaving my legal career at thirty-one. I had spent thirteen years in law, and I felt that if I did not go back, I would have to start from scratch. And what would I be able to achieve at thirty-three with fifty or sixty years to go?

Since I had left my job at the law firm, I had thrown myself into various activities. I had learned to ride a motorcycle and travel alone, repair and maintain a motorcycle, and speak Spanish. I had done this without a well-carved-out plan nor with a specific goal in mind. It had just been something that I really wanted to do. But after a year of riding a motorcycle and still without any idea of what I wanted to do when my journey was over, being in the company of someone who had dedicated her entire life to mastering one instrument had a depressing effect.

When I spoke to Michala Petri after the concert, I told her what an experience it had been to hear her play, but I also confessed that it had left me disillusioned when I thought about my own future.

"Will I ever be good at anything?" I asked her without expecting any other answer than "Yes, of course, you will." But instead, she replied: "People don't listen to my music because I have a great technique, but because I have something to say. Because I have a story to share. And it's the same for you. You also have a story to share with others; all you need is to find your instrument."

I knew she was right. I find my story in what I am passionate about. I don't have to be the best. All I need is to be true to myself. It had never occurred to me to question whether it was necessary to become the best at what I did in order to live fully. This didn't mean I wouldn't whole-heartedly take on new projects and learn to master new things. It simply meant that I could do so without the fear of failure holding me back and without the expectation of future happiness preventing me from enjoying the journey toward my goal. What joy and freedom this was!

I had equated being good at something with being happy and content. But being good at something only makes sense when I compare myself to others. Do I feel joy when I compare myself with others and feel better than them? Au contraire, the happiest moments of my life are ones when I am not aware of myself as a person. In those moments, the story about me is absent and I am at one with what I do through total involvement. The causeless joy that is always present has been given room to grow. I no longer stand in my own way, which allows me to be exactly who I am and be with what is — right here and now. It's in this that true joy and freedom are found.

AFTERWORD

> When we are unhurried and wise, we perceive that only great and worthy things have any permanent and absolute existence, – that petty fears and petty pleasures are but the shadow of reality. This is always exhilarating and sublime. By closing the eyes and slumbering, and consenting to be deceived by shows, men establish and confirm their daily life of routine and habit everywhere, which still is built on purely illusory foundations.
>
> HENRY DAVID THOREAU

On my motorcycle trip, I met many people who told me they wanted to do the same thing that I had done — most of them motivated by the desire to escape the boredom, meaninglessness, and monotony they experienced day to day.

At the beginning of my journey, I piped up and told them what they wanted to hear — which incidentally was also what I wanted to hear: that it was possible to escape the daily grind, that I was living a more exciting life than the people who stayed at home and went to work every day.

As time went on, I not only realised that it is impossible to escape the daily grind, but it isn't necessary either. The very idea that we ought to be somewhere else than where we are is precisely what prevents us from being present in our lives and discovering that we are already complete in the present locale in the present moment. There genuinely isn't anything to attain or seek outside of ourselves. Life doesn't need to be filled with adventures, but it doesn't need to exclude them either.

If I had to choose the most important lesson I learned on my travels, it would be that true happiness and freedom have no causes.

Before I left, I thought true happiness — or joy, as I like to think of it — was only something I could find outside myself, by achieving or acquiring something. Ironically, my trip taught me that quite the opposite is true. Only when I am in communion with the inner, causeless joy that is in the process of coming into being, will it indeed grow. Most importantly, I learned that freedom doesn't consist in being able to dominate or control external circumstances. On the contrary, fundamental freedom is already within all of us, and it is a matter of choosing how we relate to them.

In the same way, I thought that freedom was synonymous with a life in which I could protect myself from pain and discomfort. But I discovered the most basic condition of existence — that I cannot experience one end of the spectrum if I'm not willing to make room for the other end. By not making room for the experience of sorrow and restraint, I was excluding the feeling of joy and freedom.

Most of my life, my actions have unconsciously been an attempt either to cling to the short-term rush of pleasure (which has nothing to do with joy) or to flee from the pain inside, whether that took the form of loss, rejection, or the sense of not being good enough. None of my attempts succeeded, and the reason is that I had to be alone to make space for the pain.

Being alone as opposed to being lonely is an important distinction. Seeking other people's support and help at the time of need is a healthy sign in a person. But only I can directly be the vessel for the thoughts and directly experience the feelings and physical pain that arise in me.

Nobody else can do that for me nor can I do it for others. But once I am willing to feel the pain unconditionally – by myself – joy, untethered from causality, comes into view. The joy that is always present, no matter where I am or what is happening in and around me.

Southern Bolivia.

I still fall back into old, inappropriate reaction patterns, but it happens less often now, and when it does, I know how to steer myself free so as not to prolong the suffering – for myself or for others.

It does not take time to "find" causeless joy and freedom. It is our awareness, our fundamental being. Awareness is the stable bedrock that is always present in any experience good or bad as considered by me. It is untouched by any thought or feeling, no matter how unpleasant. Awareness is always open and never opposes what is happening. It is the backdrop against which, and from which, all thoughts, feelings, sensory impressions, and experiences arise. When I am conscious of this unchanging and ever-present foundation, I do not get confounded by external events in my life. It means I can act in ways from which I was previously cut off.

What takes time is learning to see through the veil that prevents me from being aware of causeless joy and freedom. It demands that I stop seeking stability in external everyday life and the stories I weave around it, and instead focus my attention within and let it be anchored there. It is a long and arduous struggle requiring tenacity and dedication every day. But as the Persian poet Saadi Shirazi wrote: Have patience. All things are difficult before they become easy.

ACKNOWLEDGEMENTS

There are so many people to thank for the existence of this book. In particular, I would like to express my deep gratitude:

To my family for your support and complete trust in me and for never trying to talk me out of my motorcycle adventure; to Gitte Karen Rosenqvist for your support and ability to listen in calm presence; to Mariano Calderon who ceaselessly helped and supported me in Buenos Aires – thank you for always being there for me, without you I doubt this adventure would have happened; to Roberto Baum for invaluable support in Chile; to the Ibarra family in Formosa for helping me when stranded in the middle of nowhere; to Vicky Gómez Echeverri and Camilo Perez Gomez for showing me the true beauty of Colombia and its people; to Jens Rosendal, Arturo Figueroa, Luis Rangel and Jose Luis Salazar Lara for helping me through the accident in Mexico City – your support meant nothing less than the world to me; to Chris Dawe for your endless support, help and hospitality and for introducing me to riders across the United States, many of whom are now my dear friends; to Chris Kelly – thank you for showing me what it means to share and give space to others; to Paul McLean for your hospitality, for making San Francisco my second home and for always including me; to Des Brennan for proofreading the manuscript; to Ernest Holm Svendsen for listening to me without judgment – thank you for your patience with me and honesty; to Greg Scott for encouragement and support to share my experiences in this book; to Tyge Hansen for your unwavering support and hospitality; to all my dear friends in Denmark who never forgot me while I was away; to my friends in the United States who have supported me and invited me to stay with them during later travels – a long list of people which includes Erin & Chris Ratay, Christine Hansen, Hendi Kaf, Mark Maxon, Shirah Kuschner, Kathy Dailey & Kirk Hulstrom, Jeffrey & Fabrizio Tapia, Shannon Simons, Scott Lindsay, Sharon & Stephen Burns and Francine Osikowicz & David

Roccaforte; to the BMW dealerships in the United States who took such good care of me whenever I stopped by; and to all the wonderful people I met along the way who supported me and helped me open my eyes and see the world in a different way.

Without you, none of this would have happened.

HELP SHAPE THE JOURNEY

Reviews on Amazon play a vital role in guiding others to discover wonderful books to read. If you found *The Journey to Me* enjoyable, it would mean the world to me if you could take a moment to visit the Amazon website and leave a brief, honest review.

Even the tiniest of actions can have a profound impact on the world around us.

Thank you for your support!

Printed in Great Britain
by Amazon